I WILL GO

I WILL GO

The Remarkable Story of
a Jewish Christian

Rebecca Jacobi

Christian Focus Publications

© 1993 Christian Focus Publications Ltd
ISBN 1 85792 031 7

Published by
Christian Focus Publications Ltd
Geanies House, Fearn, Ross-shire,
IV20 1TW, Scotland, Great Britain.

Printed and bound in Great Britain by
Cox & Wyman Ltd, Reading

Cover design
by
Donna Macleod

CONTENTS

Acknowledgements

I am grateful to Christian friends who have helped me concerning the writing of this book and especially to Richard Showalter of Rosedale Bible Institute, Ohio for the foreword.

Loving appreciation to my dear husband who has been a full partner in this project. It is his book, too.

I am grateful to Mrs Julie Aston for her patience in coping with my longhand manuscript and for putting it all on computer.

Praise and thanksgiving, above all, to God Himself, Father, Son and Holy Spirit, who makes all things possible in His love. This book is about Him and how He has worked. I pray that He will bless both Jew and Gentile in the reading of it.

To protect those mentioned in the book I have changed the names and places where embarrassment might be caused. Otherwise, it is as completely factual as my memory will allow.

Rebecca Jacobi

FOREWORD

When a modern Jewess sets out to follow the beckoning call of the Messiah, who could anticipate the twists and turns of the road ahead? A shocked and scandalised family, a three-month Eurasian trek in the bemused company of a half-dozen Australian adventurers, a medical and spiritual mission to India, a healing from diabetes, a son in her 'old age' - all this and much more, Rebecca Jacobi recounts with grace and verve in *I Will Go*.

No stranger to rejection and suffering, Rebecca nevertheless bears sensitive, lively witness to the power and love of God in transforming her from a stubborn, strong-willed lass to a winsome ambassador of the King. One is reminded of the words of her kinsman, Paul the apostle, 'For if the casting away of them [the Jews] be the reconciling of the world, what shall the receiving of them be, but life from the dead?' (Romans 11:15). This story is a contemporary spiritual saga brightly illuminating that 'life from the dead'.

Indeed, the transforming love of God is nowhere more profoundly and poignantly depicted than when He reaches into that community of faith which still eagerly awaits 'the Coming One' and reveals Himself in Christ as the One Who Has Come. As more and more sons and daughters of Abraham place their faith in Jesus the Messiah, the whole international family of God is blessed yet more abundantly with the fulfilment of that ancient promise to Abraham (Genesis 12:3). Hallelujah!

This is no chronicle of leisure. Rather, it is the moving story of a life heated white-hot under the merciful bellows of God, then shaped on the anvil of His grace - pommelled and pounded, yes, but always *shaped* by the Master Designer. Rebecca Jacobi's pilgrimage is not unlike that of the first Rebecca, who left her father's house in Haran by divine call to fill her role in a distant land as part of the eternal plan (Genesis 24).

To all who claim lineage from Abraham; read it. To the curious; read it. To the contented; read it. To the desperate and depressed; yes, read it. To those who enjoy a good story; read it. And thanks to God, and to Rebecca, for the partnership which produced it.

Richard Showalter
President
Rosedale Bible Institute
Irwin, Ohio

8

GLOSSARY

Adonai (Hebrew)
Means 'our Master' or 'Lord'. One of the names for God.

Dietary Laws of the Jews
Most Jews, in some way, observe the various food laws. These are based on the Bible's Book of Leviticus, where there is a long list of permitted and forbidden animals, fish and birds. Only those animals which both chew the cud and are cloven-footed (such as cows and sheep), can be eaten. Pigs, rabbits and horses are forbidden. Fish must have both scales and fins (such as salmon, trout and haddock). Those which do not (such as shellfish and eels) must not be eaten. Birds of prey, such as eagles and partridges may not be eaten, but those which eat seed are permitted, e.g. chicken and ducks. A further ruling states that meat and milk products cannot be eaten together. This means that Jews do not have milk in their drinks or cream on their desserts after a meat meal, and do not use butter on meat sandwiches.

Hasham (Hebrew)
Means 'the name'. Used by Orthodox Jews as a substitute for the word 'God' in ordinary conversation.

Hassidic
A Jew belonging to Hassidism. It is a Jewish mystical

movement which grew from the teaching of Baal Shem Tov in the 18th Century. It is an ultra-orthodox group, but it stresses the importance of prayer and uses chanting and dancing in aid to communication with God.

High Holy Days
Special occasions for the Jews, such as Jewish New Year (Rosh Hashanah), the Day of Atonement (Yom Kippur), the Feast of Tabernacles (Succot), the Festival of Lights (Hanukah), the Passover (Pesach).

Kosher
Food fulfilling the requirements of the Jewish law.

Messiah
The Anointed One. The Christ. Jesus of Nazareth is the Messiah.

Messianic Jew
A Jew who has turned to Jesus as Messiah.
A Hebrew Christian who acknowledges Jesus to be the Son of God.

Orthodox Judaism
Orthodox Jews believe that the Torah is the Word of God, given directly by God and written down by Moses, whereas most non-Orthodox Jews believe it is also a human document. In Orthodox synagogues men and women sit separately. This is done because women sat apart in the ancient Temple. Women in the Orthodox synagogues do not play any leading role. Hebrew is used in Orthodox synagogues. There is no use of musical instruments on

Sabbaths or during festivals. To play music would be regarded as 'work'.

Passover (Pesach)
A Jewish spring festival commemorating the deliverance of the Israelites from bondage in Egypt.

Rabbi
A Jewish scholar or teacher, especially of the law.

Sabbath
The weekly day of rest and worship instituted at the Creation (Gen.2.3). N.B.: Shabbat is the Hebrew word for Sabbath.

Yeshua (Joshua)
The Hebrew name for Jesus.

SPEAKING A DIFFERENT LANGUAGE

Certain words have different meanings for the British and Americans. The list below will hopefully avoid confusion when reading *I Will Go*.

BRITISH	AMERICAN
Sweets	Candy
Cheque	Check
Biscuits	Cookies
Nappy	Diaper
Lift	Elevator
Autumn	Fall
Torch	Flashlight
Jam	Jelly
Handbag	Purse
Public School	Private School
Railway	Railroad
Prep	Homework or preparatory work
Holiday(s)	Vacation
Hospital ward	Unit Ward
Ward Sister	Unit Manager
Staff Nurse	Charge Nurse
Matron	Chief Administrator of a hospital
Toilet	Bathroom
Post	Mail
Fourth floor	Fifth floor
Garden	Yard
Car	Automobile
Petrol	Gas
Trousers	Pants
Wash oneself	Wash up
Tights	Pantyhose

PREFACE

Why was I, a defiant and rebellious Orthodox Jewess, seated week by week for several months in the crowded gallery of a large London city church? Unbeknown to me, at that stage in my life God's grace was at work. This became evident at 7.22 p.m. on the 22nd August 1962, when I was confronted by none other than Jesus the Messiah Himself, who challenged me to follow Him. When my namesake, Rebecca, was asked by her family if she would become the bride of Isaac she said, without a moment's hesitation, "I will go." When the vision came to me in that gallery my response was the same. I would go with Him wherever He would lead.

The promise to follow this Jewish Jesus, the true Messiah, eventually led to my being ostracised during my seventeenth year by my Ultra-Orthodox Jewish family and virtually the whole South London Hebrew community.

At the age of eighteen I began my nurse's training at a well-known London hospital. I felt no sense of 'calling'. I just needed a job with accommodation and a friend agreed to give me a fiver (a lot of money in the '60's) if I stuck it out for six months! I qualified *three years* later! Midwifery training and Bible college followed. This led to an overland trek to India accompanied by six burly Australian young men! Three and a half years of being an evangelist-cum-medical worker in Western India brought joys as well as failures, set-backs as well as problems. Only God's grace made it work and I owe a great debt of gratitude to Him who is completely faithful.

God permitted the door to India to become closed to me and, like a spoilt child, I behaved badly. Have you ever watched such a child when they cannot get their own way? They kick and scream, occasionally throwing themselves to the ground. God allowed me to behave in a foolish way. He allowed me to fall down, but He also picked me up, disciplined me and never for one moment stopped loving me.

As I reflect on my life I remember A. W. Tozer's words, 'If it is good God did it. And if it is bad I did it.'

Spiritually, everything was just fine, or so I thought. God was blessing me and, in a small way, He appeared to be using me to extend His kingdom, usually through the occasions when I was invited to give my testimony. I was riding high, but like Dagon of old I was about to 'fall off my perch'! The Lord knew that there were many areas in my life which needed correction and He proceeded to straighten me out. What a task!

He began one Lord's Day in 1981. I was sitting alone in the morning service. I was singing along with the rest of the congregation that delightful chorus *He lives! He lives! Christ Jesus lives today*. The service had not officially started and a few people were still taking their places in the remaining seats. A complete stranger sat on the empty chair beside me.

After the service I greeted her and asked if she was new to the area. When she told me she was from Germany I realised that we had things in common. I told her how my dad's family originally came from Germany but left in a hurry because of the Anti-Semitic movement which was breaking out there. She looked uneasy - so ill at ease that I asked her if she was alright.

I was astounded when she told me her job during the war was as a wardress in Belsen. She was the one who ushered Jews into the gas chambers - thousands of Jewish women, including those who were clutching little children in their arms. She, now a Christian, did not have time to finish her sentence, for I harshly silenced the sound of her voice with a *very* angry retort.

On my way home I saw her waiting for a bus that was not likely to come for another couple of hours because of the poor Sunday service. She flagged me down and asked for a lift in my car. I gave full vent to my anger.

"Fraulein, *you* made my people walk to their deaths. *Now* you can walk!"

I drove off, leaving her standing still at the bus stop.

One chapter in this book deals with the outcome of the situation as a whole, but bitterness of spirit was not the only thing from which I needed to be healed. I was a diabetic dependent on insulin injections and a carbohydrate controlled diet. God even allowed me to be a fool, for I once ended up in a Police cell. This tea-totaller had an insulin coma and it was confused with being 'drunk and disorderly'! God manifested His mighty power and touched this, His beloved child. A miracle took place confusing some medical minds!

Perhaps one of the loveliest happenings in my life was my marriage to Mark. God has blessed us in more ways than it is possible for me to recount although we have had our problems - just as you probably have. God's grace has made everything beautiful for us, not least the joy of our only son born to us in 1984.

"What of your Jewish family?" you may ask. "Is it a 'happy ever after' story?"

My Rabbinic grandfather apparently experienced a deathbed conversion. Oh, that I had been there! As for my parents... well, read the book!

"Why don't you write a book about all this?" asked several of my well-meaning friends.

I committed it to the Lord but it took me a while to get to grips with the idea. May He be glorified as you read my story - the pilgrimage of a Hebrew Christian, a Messianic Jewess. May God bless you.

1

THE FAMILY

"Say unto Zion, 'You are my People'."
(Isaiah 51:16)

My father, mother, brother and I all lived with my mother's
father in a smart Jewish area of London. My beloved,
elderly grandfather was a Rabbi in an Ultra-Orthodox
Jewish synagogue situated just about a Sabbath mile from
our home. He wore a black, fur-trimmed hat, a black knee-
length coat and his black trousers always looked as if they
had fought with his shoes!

Orthodox synagogues do not use musical instruments
on Sabbaths or during festivals. Instead, they have a man
who is the Cantor. My grandfather was the Cantor Rabbi.
He sang with great passion about the Holy One and the
sufferings of our people Israel.

Both my grandfather's mother and father were deaf and
dumb. As a result of their handicaps, they could not find
any employment. To help combat their subsequent poverty they clandestinely made their own beer and, by night,
friends and neighbours purchased the illicit brew. In 1879
they decided that they should 'come out into the open' and
market it. The business was started down in the cold, damp
cellar of their slum dwelling, and, to their surprise and
pleasure, it quickly began to flourish. In 1880 new premises
were obtained. Their little brewery soon turned into a large

commercial empire and is still well known (and sampled!) to this day.

Their rapidly-acquired wealth naturally provided a very fine education for Grandfather and his brother Fred at the famous Eton College. His younger sister Agnes was educated privately in a schoolroom at home by a stern old governess called Miss Rosenberg.

After the deaths of my great-grandparents, Grandfather and Fred naturally inherited the entire business. Agnes was left a large amount of money and she promptly used it to set up her own business which was also a brewery - the only trade she knew!

Whilst still fairly young, Grandfather and Fred both experienced the horrors of the First World War.

Grandfather, a Colonel, was completely in the thick of a series of terrible battles. He vowed that, if God spared him, then, when all the fighting was over, he would serve the one true God. He not only survived but was decorated with the Military Cross for bravery in the Battle of the Somme.

Peace was restored in 1918 and he immediately became a Rabbinic student, so devoting his life to God, as he had promised.

In 1925 Fred decided to sell his share of the brewery. Grandfather snapped it up. Fred was then able to afford to emigrate to Canada where he later started his own success-ful business enterprise - a chain of many launderettes beginning in Toronto and spreading to almost every major town and city out there.

This obviously left Grandfather as the sole owner of his late parents' brewery and a man of great wealth. It fol-lowed that the 18th Century house in which we lived was a large one, probably containing around fifteen bedrooms.

Grandfather was a widower and missed his wife desperately. She was named Martha, but everyone called her Polly. When they met she was a pretty, young Jewish girl with a mop of dark curly hair and amazingly big sparkling hazel green eyes. She had come to London in 1919 from Dublin's 'Fair City' specifically to marry my tall, handsome grandfather in 1920. I never knew my quick tempered Irish granny, for she died at the age of 45 years in 1945 - a year prior to my birth. Her last year was spent racked with pain due to a carcinoma. Even though her death was expected, it was nevertheless a blow to the whole family, but especially to her husband.

Grandfather's brewery was eventually taken over by a firm which I will call Levi-Stein Breweries. Miss Agnes Stein was Grandfather's sister and my great-aunt - an awesome woman!

I remember when I was only about four or five years old being taken to visit her. She had previously suffered a fall, thereby fracturing her right hip. Now I was amazed to see that Great-aunt Agnes was balding. Her ginger coloured wig was balanced on the knob at the foot of her big brass bed. The wig's parting looked machine stitched and there was not a hair out of place. I wanted to touch it, but I did not dare!

Mum had told me previously that some wives of Hassidic Jewish Rabbis covered their heads with a wig so that only their husbands saw their real hair. Miss Stein was not married and yet she had a wig. This was all so confusing to my young mind!

During his late sixties Grandfather found it impossible to get around due to the advancement of diabetic gangrene in both his feet. This resulted in below-the-knee amputations at St. Anthony's Hospital, Cheam, Surrey.

Jews fear assimilation, but he did not mind the Roman Catholics who owned and worked the hospital, for they never consciously tried to convert him to their religion. They said he was of God's chosen race and so, spiritually, they left him alone.

However, one person took a different view - his barber who visited him every few weeks to trim his hair and tidy his long, bushy beard. This barber was a member of the Christian Brethren, sometimes known as the Plymouth Brethren. He was a fine and enthusiastic Christian who was not afraid to speak out for what he believed. He held the view that people of all nations, including the Jews, needed to hear about God's salvation in Christ. So he used the opportunities to tell my grandfather that Jesus was indeed the true Messiah. I believe that the faithful witnessing of the barber probably resulted in my grandfather accepting the Lord Yeshua as his Saviour and Messiah on his death-bed years later.

I missed Grandfather's companionship much of the time and began to experience true feelings of loneliness.

Dad tried to jolly me along throughout Grandfather's absence. Sometimes he would take me to Wimbledon Common where we would ride our two chestnut horses which were stabled at the Dog and Fox Riding School. Other times we tried to catch small fish from the ponds, or just kicked a football around. However, in those days he worked fairly long hours for a firm of Jewish accountants and so I remained quite lonely. At that stage in my life I was still an only child and there were few other local Jewish children of my age with whom to play.

Dad was brought up in an Orthodox Jewish family in Berlin where they were comfortably off financially. Dad's father was an eminent surgeon and his mother was a dutiful wife to her husband. She bore him Albert, Solomon, Ruth, Miriam and Rudi.

By the end of December 1938, the Nazis either took away or destroyed nearly all their material possessions and my paternal grandfather was placed on the 'wanted' list by the German S.S. A foolish slip of the tongue put Grandfather and his family into great danger. Dancing with Grandfather at a smart social function which was attended by friends and neighbours, a woman asked him what he thought of the changing times. Very unwisely he said that the 'little Corporal' should be assassinated. Not all the neighbours were their friends and such a remark coming from a Jew about Hitler was regarded as high treason.

Many of their friends were either missing or in hiding. Others were in labour camps. Jewish children were being rounded up at gunpoint. The Jews were the major victims of the persecution. So, at the beginning of 1939, my grandfather decided to flee with his wife and five children to England before they too went missing or were killed.

Having tried in vain to obtain employment in England through the 'Situations Wanted' columns of the better and older national newspapers, they eventually resorted to flight. Spending all he had to obtain forged papers and passports, they set out on the hazardous journey to England. Although the full details of the journey are no longer remembered, part of the escape was made by hiding in wooden crates, complete with air holes, in a goods train that took them over the border and into France. From there a woman who was called Matilda arranged for their passage to England. She had access to a house in Windsor. After a short stay there with Auntie Matty, as they called her, she found the family permanent accommodation in Dundonald Road, Wimbledon.

In September 1939, when the Second World War broke out, the family were treated with suspicion. German people were branded as 'enemy aliens' and my grandfather was interned on the Isle of Man. A large white swastika was crudely painted on the front of their rented English terraced house, presumably by their so-called neighbours who wrongly suspected them of being German spies. Not all Londoners were unkind to them. One Gentile family who knew that, with Grandfather away, the family had hardly any money, faithfully gave them a food parcel every Friday afternoon, enabling them to celebrate their Jewish Sabbath.

In 1941, when my dad was just eighteen years old, he was nationalised and, soon after, he enlisted as a soldier with the British Army.

Dad had previously met my mother at a local dance. Several dates followed the original meeting and my Auntie Miriam, now in her late seventies, remembers them as a couple well suited to each other and who were hopelessly in love!

Before being posted overseas Dad married Mum at the Synagogue in Worple Road, Wimbledon. The pretty, young bride and her groom stood beneath a 'Huppa' (canopy) which was decorated with red roses and white carnations from my maternal grandmother's lovely flower gardens. The couple then drank wine and promised to uphold the Jewish religion in their new life together. The groom gave the bride her wedding ring and said a special

Hebrew vow of faithfulness. The `Ketubah' (marriage certificate) was read and signed by them. Finally, the groom crushed the wine glass beneath his foot. This is always performed by Jewish bridegrooms, probably in memory of the destruction of the Temple. It may also be done to denote that there will be both fortune and misfortune together as a married couple.

My father requested leave for his wedding but, at the last moment, it was not granted, so he went A.W.O.L. from His Majesty's forces in order to marry his bride. Neither she nor the guests at the wedding knew about his misdemeanour. The shock was to come later!

Because it was war-time the newlyweds could not go to exotic, far-away places for their honeymoon. They had to be content to borrow my Uncle Joseph's apartment in Wimbledon Hill for a while - in fact for a much shorter time than planned, for their honeymoon was unceremoniously cut short by the arrival of the Military Police! At 4.30 a.m. their sleep was disturbed by two huge men in red caps hammering loudly with their fists on the door of the apartment. The bewildered young bride was left behind as her groom was whisked away to a Detention Centre for Military Offenders, otherwise known as 'the glass house', where, amongst other things, he whitewashed coal for a punishment!

The Regimental Sergeant Major shouted at my father, "First we get Hitler - then we get *you*!"

Active service followed. Dad was posted overseas to fight in the desert campaign. In 1942 he was captured by the Germans and then the Nazi nightmare followed for him.

When his captors at the Prisoner of War camp realised

that he was Jewish, arrangements were immediately made to send him to a Concentration Camp. As he arrived in enemy occupied Europe, he was bundled with many more prisoners into a filthy, overcrowded railway wagon. There was a sense of terror in their hearts as the train, in blackout, rumbled through the night. Dad was very frightened indeed.

The train halted at its destination and he was shoved by the butt of a German gun out on to the platform. Auschwitz! Men, women and children (some very young) were made to walk along an icy, unmade road. They walked and walked. The road seemed endless, and was for some - those who stumbled were shot through the head or savaged by German Shepherd dogs.

At the death camp, my father was stripped of his clothes and issued with prison clothing. He owned one thin, grey blanket for warmth, but he was desperately cold and, like nearly all the other prisoners, acquired more clothing only when someone died. One morning he awoke to find that the man in the upper bunk had died of typhoid in the night. Father stole the dead man's infected clothing and meagre bread ration - after all, the dead had no need of these things and he needed to survive. Once he found some grass which sprang up in the mud. He ate it quickly before anyone else had the chance. During his time in the camps, he saw people shot, gassed, burned or die from starvation. Typhoid claimed the lives of so many - the elderly and the infants were always the first to die. Rats, fleas and leeches plagued the living constantly.

Dad now describes it as 'all hell let loose on earth'. He says that he often thought of escape, but it was only ever a thought. I once asked him why he did not try, for there were only a few German guards compared with the vast number of interned Jews. My father explained that other guards were recruited from among the Jewish prisoners who, in order to survive themselves, played a part in the destruction of their own people. The prisoners hated the Jewish traitors more than they hated the German guards.

So how did my father survive his stay in two German death camps - Auschwitz and Belsen?

When he first arrived at Auschwitz some of the older captives who were helping with the disembarkation whispered to him, "Say you have a trade."

"But I haven't a trade," muttered Dad.

"You 'ave now, mate. You're a cobbler with me!" said the prisoner next to him, giving him a gentle shove.

This helpful employment played a part in keeping Dad alive, for those without a trade were some of the earliest to be shepherded to the gas chambers.

A day came in Belsen when, near total collapse from starvation and the hard graft of breaking large rocks, Dad heard a commotion. All of the German guards looked scared stiff. Dad could not understand what was happening. There were groups of Jewish prisoners on their knees fearlessly and openly blessing God; behaviour which was punishable by death.

The Americans had arrived! The ordeal was over! Some American soldiers vomited at the sights in the camp - others could hardly tolerate the overpowering smell of death and decay. However, wonder of wonders, for the survivors it had, at last, all come to an end.

Six million Jews were mercilessly killed by the Nazis from 1939 to 1945. One million of those were young children and babies. Dad lived, but he was transformed during his time in the camp from a fit, healthy young man into a quivering, frail being who could hardly shuffle along. At the age of 22 years, he weighed only 91 pounds.

When the camp was liberated, he was sent to a British military base in North Wales where he was nursed back to health. It was from there that he wrote:

Pwllheli,
North Wales
31st August, 1945

My dearest Wife,

This letter may come as a shock to you, but I am alive!!! I have been informed that you received a telegram three years ago telling you that I was 'missing, believed killed.' What must you have thought? After all these years you have probably considered yourself to be a war widow. Well, my darling, I am alive!

Three years ago I was captured by the Germans and I was thrown into two death camps. If the Americans hadn't come when they did then I honestly think that I would have died. It has been hell. Physically, it is over now - thank God. But the dreams are still with me; terrible nightmares which make me to dread sleep.

I am here in North Wales recovering and I will be coming home *very* soon. *I cannot wait to see you.* I have thought about you almost non-stop. I did write to you from the camps but the letters obviously didn't get through to you. The 'pigs' won't have posted them; any letters would have been destroyed, I expect.

I cannot wait to see you and be with you. I long to hold you. You will see a great change in me. I am *very* thin and I have a job walking well without help, but I am getting better and we will resume a normal life one day soon.

I love you so much.

Your ever loving husband,
Rudi

My mother sat down slowly in a chair as she read the letter. She read it over and over again several times. It was the first line of communication she had received from him. Rudi was alive? Alive? What should she do? She really believed during the previous year that he was dead. After the telegram arrived from the War Office she was in a daze, refusing to believe that he was dead. Whatever anyone else said, she refused to believe that her husband was not alive. However, as time went on, she decided to come to terms with being a war widow and her sister persuaded her to 'come out of her shell' and 'live a little'.

Eleven months prior to the receipt of her husband's unexpected letter she had met another man who had become her lover. What should she do now? How should she handle the situation?

"Well, you don't really have a choice, do you, honey? You'll have to tell your boyfriend that it is all over. You have a husband, after all!" advised her sister. "If I were you I'd get up to North Wales right now and see Rudi."

"Travel isn't very easy now," replied my mother making excuses. "And what will I tell my boyfriend?"

"Leave him to me. I'll go and see him for you and explain. Okay?" said her sister, giving her a hug.

Their conversation was interrupted by an unexpected knock on the door.

"Who could that be? I'll answer it," called my mother, walking through the hall.

She opened the door. Her eyes widened, she gasped and her hand covered her mouth. She felt her heart miss a beat. My father stood there with his arms outstretched. She threw her arms around him and could not let go of him. Tears of joy ran down their faces and they kissed away each other's salty tears.

"Oh, Rudi, Rudi," whispered my mother.

"I'm back, my darling. I'm back for good," Dad laughed and cried at the same time, still holding her as tightly as he could. "Aren't you going to let me in? Am I to stay on the doorstep?"

"Who is it?" called my mother's sister, walking towards the front door.

When she saw my parents embracing she put her arms around the pair and led them into the house. She was horrified to see the appalling physical condition of her brother-in-law and covered up her embarrassment by saying to him, "Well, I suppose I'll have to be the one to organise a welcome home party. You should have warned us that you were coming and we would have saved up our food coupons!"

All that mattered to the couple was that they were together again - forever!

I was born in 1946. My brother was born eight years later in 1954.

At my brother's birth the whole family celebrated and congratulated my parents on having a son. They themselves rejoiced greatly over having a boy. David's birth and circumcision were truly marked occasions. He was circumcised by the Mohel - a specially trained Rabbi. I remember when the Mohel arrived. All the men were in the main living room with this little baby boy and all the women were waiting silently outside in the hall.

My mother jumped as she heard her new baby yell. She could hear the shrill screams and was helpless to do anything to comfort him. Still tired from the birth of her baby, she buried her head in her lap and wept. Her sister-in-law tried to comfort her, but Mother just shook her off. The door slowly opened. There was the Mohel holding baby David out for his mother. She quickly took hold of her precious little bundle and sat rocking him to and fro until the high pitched cries turned to just a snuffly whimper.

"It is God's blessing that you have such a fine, healthy son, m'dear," said the Mohel to Mother in a strong Yiddish accent. She just nodded, smiling through her tears.

Eight years later she rocked backwards and forwards alone. Her son was gone forever. He was not there to cuddle or to scold. My parents sat together as if in a daze as the paediatrician at Great Ormond Street Children's Hospital pronounced, "I am afraid that we could do no more for David. The Hodgkin's Disease just took control. I really am sorry." David was dead. Dead? They could not believe what they were hearing.

My parents never seemed to recover from the death of my little brother. Their grief was like an ulcer that would not heal. It was awful for us all, but another 'living hell' for them.

2

A SEARCH FOR GOD

Convent school! (1954-1959)

Most youngsters enjoy their schooldays from the first, but there are some who for social, rather than educational, reasons have found them rather difficult. At the age of eight years I was sent to a Roman Catholic Girls' fee paying school because it was well known for its high standards of educational achievement. It was a large boarding school situated in the heart of Surrey and run by a teaching order of nuns. How sad it was for me to wave good-bye to my family, including my newly born baby brother David at the beginning of September, 1954, and say, "I will see you in December." I doubt if any experience faced as an adult is ever likely to surpass that which confronted me, having left the shelter of a Jewish home for the first time, and being plunged into this new environment.

I used to cry a lot due to homesickness and, on one occasion, I did try to escape from the Convent. I was very frightened and most unhappy. I resented Grandfather paying the fees. I wanted to go home. I also felt as though my family were getting rid of me and replacing me with my baby brother. I was cross and jealous.

I was friendless at first because of my Jewishness. The Roman Catholic pupils found it a bit odd, to say the least, to have a Jewess in the Convent and would call after me,

"You killed Jesus! You killed Jesus! Jew-girl! Jew-girl!"

I developed stomach pains and headaches which were obviously manifestations of my distress and symptoms of my inward isolation and loneliness. A nun linked me with another more sympathetic pupil and suddenly I had a friend. I began to regain my confidence and others became more interested in me as a person. There was give and take on both sides. I had dared to venture forth. The battle was half over. My eyes were no longer glazed and dull, but bright and laughing.

Nevertheless, I found it almost impossible to fully practise my Jewishness, but I did try by not eating shell-fish, pork, bacon, ham and by not drinking milk at the same meal when I had eaten meat. Hardly any of the school meals could be remotely regarded as Kosher, which worried both me and my family. I tried desperately hard to keep the Jewish Sabbath by praying Jewish prayers. It was difficult, for few Roman Catholics understood my Jewish ways.

Despite such problems I was happily living in a world full of interest and colour. I was no longer retreating from my new environment but instead I was advancing to meet it.

I did fairly well academically and began to really love my time at the school. I enjoyed everything except Religious Studies. The mixture of Judaism and Roman Catholicism seemed to curdle within me. When I was not quite thirteen I decided to give up absolutely all private religious observances. I felt that if I did not keep Shabbat, the High Holy Days and what I considered to be all the petty laws, then no thunderbolt would come from the 'big blue yonder' and strike me dead.

"After all," I thought, "there are many Jews who are not religious but who are still very aware of their Jewish roots. Many Jewish people do not fulfil their duties to the letter, so I will not fulfil mine!"

On voicing this decision, first to the nuns and then to my family, it was decided by my grandfather that I should become a weekly boarder so that I would be at home for Shabbat. Religious observances and family life were very important to my family and these two factors, they felt, needed to be instilled into me. Therefore, every Friday I was collected from the Convent School and driven home by my father in his shiny, black Austin Seven automobile, forcing me to share in the Jewish Sabbath, whether I liked it or not! I was then returned safe and sound to school on the Sunday just in time for tea, which always consisted of hot buttered toast, freshly baked scones, home-made strawberry jam, thick double cream and cups of steaming hot tea!

Where are you, God? (1961)

After about two years of being a 'weekly boarder' I began, at weekends, to meet up with a Jewish teenage group. Most of us were 'just good friends', for we had grown up together in the same Jewish area. Many of our parents were friends, too, mainly through the religious services and social events that took place at the synagogue.

If there was time after the Sabbath was over, I would meet up with my friends in the 'Orinoco Coffee Bar'. We would talk for what seemed hours over a cup of frothy, expresso coffee. If the Sabbath ended too late then we would meet up in our homes. Always we discussed such evocative subjects as politics, the Peace Movement, how to put the world to rights, and religion.

I was very confused about the existence of God and listened carefully to what the others in the group had to say about a 'Supreme Being'. After a while, I tried to find Him by measuring up to the standards set by the Ten Commandments. Surely if I lived a good life then God, if He existed, would reveal Himself to me. The religious guideposts made morality a fairly uncomplicated business as it clearly assessed my conduct as either good or bad.

Sin, I understood, was a failure to live up to the standard, but the way Roman Catholics handled their moral failures differed greatly from the way I had to cope. They did not all seem to take failure too seriously but went to the confessional, got it off their chests and carried on. I knew only too well about the Day of Atonement, which took place in the autumn of each year, when Jews repented of their sins and sought forgiveness. However, in my case, I seemed to repress my guilt and carry it about with me. I did wonder whether God was to be found in other religions, but this was most certainly discouraged by my family and, in those days, people were not encouraged to investigate other faiths. One of the nuns who taught religion to the girls in our school warned them against investigation of my Jewishness! She said that, if they did, it would be a horrible sin and an appropriate punishment would follow. My Roman Catholic friend, Susan, did show some interest in Judaism and I stupidly wondered whether lightning would strike her for disobeying the nun's instructions. I was glad nothing happened!

"You ought to be searching for God in your own religion," said my Orthodox Jewish Uncle Solomon. "It has a great deal to offer you. You don't have to switch from Judaism to something else to find spiritual fulfilment. You could begin again by going to a Sabbath service or two just once in a while!"

I felt as though the search in that direction had gone on long enough, so I disregarded his advice.

Chatting with some upper sixth-formers, who were obviously both older and more sophisticated than the girls in my age group, I noticed that they seemed to be moving away from the religion of their childhood. Some had travelled to exotic places, seen other cultures and acquired a tolerance for other peoples' customs. They had begun to explore their own sexuality in a less puritanical way and were throwing off the constraints of their religious upbringing. What they had to say was fascinating, but nothing was of any real help in my search for God.

Sometimes I felt very Jewish; at other times I felt myself to be 'something else'. What I was sure of was my need to find something or Someone to believe in. I felt that there must be a Power behind the universe, and there must be a meaning for my life here on earth and beyond in eternity. My search was causing me to stay awake at night and I felt weary during the daytime. If there was anyone 'up there' then why did He not manifest Himself to me?

Walking through the Convent's garden one day I picked, with permission from an old nun who was gardening, a most beautiful rose. I fingered gently the soft pink petals and concluded that man could not make such a lovely thing; neither did it just happen. The God whom I was seeking must be responsible for Creation. I took the flower into the Convent's simple, but beautiful, little chapel. There was a smell of stale incense pervading the place. A tear trickled down my face as I looked at the plain wooden cross hanging above the altar. I wanted to be alone to think about the One who surely made my rose.

"Oh, where are You, God?" I whispered. "Where are You? I am trying to find You. If You really do exist then please make Yourself known to me."

One of the Irish nuns walked quietly into the chapel and was amazed to find me, of all people, praying there! After crossing herself she sat down beside me in the pew. I felt deeply annoyed because she was invading my personal space. I wanted to shout at her and make her go away. Instead, I gave a big sigh and looked upwards.

"If you weren't a flippin' Jewess, my girl, you'd make a lovely Catholic, to be sure," she said, giving me a friendly nudge. Thankfully, she took the hint and went to the back of the chapel in order to tidy the piles of hymn books before leaving.

Alone again, my mind returned to the all important issue of God. If He existed, then did He love me? I really needed to know. If there was no God, then what hope did I have? What a dilemma!

The Invitation (1962)

A group of us were at the back of the class reading 'selections' from *Lady Chatterley's Lover* by D. H. Lawrence. We were supposed to be engaged in a science lesson!

The Science Mistress was a student teacher. She was also a Protestant! Her Teachers' Training College sent her to the Convent by mistake and the following week she was to be transferred to the correct school for her teaching practice.

"Rebecca, bring out what you are doing!"

I was nearly sixteen years old but I felt as if she was

treating me like a naughty little child.

"Rebecca! Did you hear what I said?"

"Yes, Miss," I replied.

"What shall I do?" I whispered to my classmate Wendy.

"She's religious," replied the girl, "so take her out this Bible and tell her you were reading from it."

"I can't," I said, shaking my head. "I'd be lying."

"Rebecca, how long do I have to wait?" called the Mistress.

"Who does she think she is? Mother Superior?" whispered my classmate, again thrusting a Catholic Bible into my hand and giving me a shove towards the front of the class.

I walked forward with the Bible, turning once to look back at my friends who were giggling behind their desk lids.

"I was reading from this, Miss," I lied.

"So from which part of this Bible were you reading?" she asked, drumming her fingers on her desk.

I smirked and turned back once again, grinning in the direction of my supportive friends and having no answer to give her.

"When you have decided from what part of the Bible you were reading, let me know - and before 'prep', girl, do you hear?"

"Huh! I won't," I said defiantly.

"Oh, but you will," came her sharp reply.

I returned to my seat, muttering to my friends that I did not think much of her and referred to her as 'bossy madam'.

When all the other pupils were at 'prep', I sloped off to see the student teacher who was thankfully alone in the classroom and where I knew I would not be overheard by my friends who would think I was a 'creep'.

"I hadn't been reading from the Bible. I lied to you and so I apologise for that alone. Nothing else!" I said, even more firmly than before, standing as tall as possible - a good three inches above her, which I hoped would give me an air of superiority.

I moved towards the door but she sat down and signalled, in a friendly way, for me to do the same. I declined, and remained standing - very much on my guard.

"Do you read the Bible, Rebecca?"

I shook my head. I was not going to allow her to slice into my soul.

"Would you like to come to Bethel Evangelical Church with me on Sunday?" she asked, and then continued, "I have been a member there since becoming a Christian two years ago. It's super!"

I shook my head. I wondered what she meant by 'becoming a Christian'. I considered it an odd remark for anyone to make. I never heard the nuns speak in such a way. I thought that to 'become a Christian' meant that one had to be christened in the Roman Catholic Church!

"Why not?" she persisted.

"You are making me miss 'prep' and the nun who is the Mistress of Discipline will put detention on me for it. So can I go now, please?" I said, with a sigh, raising my eyes heavenwards.

I was excused. Just as I reached the door to leave the class room, I turned back and said, "I am Jewish."

"Please ask your parents, Becky, if you can come on Sunday," she called after me. "I would love you to come and I am sure that you would enjoy it."

During the following Sabbath, things were getting a bit boring for me. Mother and I had ceremoniously lit the candles and said the Hebrew prayer, so welcoming in the Jewish Sabbath.

Once the hearty Sabbath meal was finished, a middle-aged Gentile woman was busily washing up. (We employed her so that we did not break the Sabbath by unnecessary work). The noise of dishes being stacked in the nearby kitchen could just be heard.

Grandfather was sleeping off the very fine food and was snoring gently. He looked so peaceful and comfortable in his big leather rocking chair.

My parents were talking in another room about my young brother David. They were very anxious as he was seriously ill with Hodgkin's Disease in Great Ormond Street Hospital.

I felt excluded by the family and decided to sneak out of the house. Life was surely much more exciting for a teenager outside. However, I was suddenly stopped in my tracks by the Gentile woman who entered the room to switch on our electric lights. The sudden illumination disturbed Grandfather and he awoke with one loud snore - he sounded like something going wrong in a sawmill!

"Where are you going, my dear?" he asked me, rubbing his eyes.

"Nowhere, Grandfather," I lied with a sigh, sitting down again.

Having been made to stay with the family, I decided I would liven up the occasion. Remembering the school teacher's invitation, I asked him if I could attend Bethel Evangelical Church on the Sunday.

"My life! You want to do *what*?" asked my grandfather, raising his voice and looking angrily at me.

His shouting brought my parents back into the room.

"Whatever is going on? Why are you upsetting your grandfather?" Mother asked me.

"I only asked if I could go to a Christian church with a student teacher on Sunday. That's all," I told my mother.

She retorted, "What do you mean 'that's all'?"

"She will bring disgrace upon Israel. After all, she is of Abraham's seed," said the old Rabbi, furiously rocking backwards and forwards in his chair.

"Be quiet, Dad," snapped my mother, sharply.

"Are you mad?" my father asked me at the top of his voice.

Mother was determined that she would settle the matter.

"Have you taken leave of your senses? What are you trying to do to us? You're just being plain awkward. You are not going! Do you hear? Becky! Rebecca! Do you hear me?" yelled my mother, frustrated by my calm and lack of response. "We have enough worries with David so don't cause us any more problems, girl."

"You are a Jewish girl, Rebecca. You are not going and that's the end of the matter!" shouted my father at the top of his voice as he banged his fists hard on the table, making the remaining cutlery jump.

So I went!

"Bethel" - The house of God (1962)

I met the student teacher and her Christian friend at a main London railway station and we walked briskly along from there to Bethel Evangelical Church just in time for the 10.30 a.m. service, which, incidentally, included a sermon that lasted over an hour! I wondered how people could sit for so long listening in silence to one elderly man. It was in stark contrast to synagogue worship where one is often free to move around and chat. When the service was over, lunch was served on the premises. The conversation at the meal table was almost exclusively about Christianity and I felt left out once again.

I had not realised when I accepted the invitation that it was a full day's programme. After lunch we took a long walk around a London park and then we assembled in one of the church rooms where the minister's wife was leading a women's Bible study. Most of the behatted ladies were well into their 60's and the student teacher, her friend and I, were the only young ones there.

Tea followed. This led up to the evening service which to me, as a non-Christian teenager, was even more of a drag than the morning service! After the long evening service there followed a time of fellowship, when people stood around in groups talking about Christian doctrine and drinking luke-warm, milky coffee. Mine had a skin on the top.

I hated it all. I found it totally boring and I was glad to return home again.

"Well, Becky, did you like it with that teacher woman at that church?" asked my dad from behind his Sunday paper.

"Yes, and I am going again next week. It was wonderful," I lied, not prepared to admit defeat.

Grandfather prayed that I would not bring dishonour upon Israel again, but my mother snapped at him, telling him to 'shut up'. And he did.

I repeated the morning services, lunches, walks, Bible

studies, teas, evening services and the lukewarm coffees for Sunday after Sunday.

My family suspected that I was only going to Bethel Evangelical Church out of sheer rebellion against them; and maybe I was. However, my new found Christian friends were encouraged by my regular attendance at the church and believed I was 'getting keen'!

One Sunday evening, after having been told a couple of times by well-meaning Christians, 'You need to accept Jesus into your life as your Saviour,' I decided enough was enough! I made up my mind there and then that I would never attend that church again - or any church, come to that! As for the synagogue, I would only go along if there was a Bar Mitzvah, a wedding or one of the High Holy days - and then only if there was a 'bit of a do' afterwards.

I sat in what I vowed would be my last ever evening service. I was so bored, I decided to pass the time by reading from a book which had been left on the pew in front of me. After all, it was surely preferable to counting organ pipes!

I picked up the book in a slow, quiet way so that I would not disturb the rest of the congregation who all seemed totally enthralled by the preacher's lengthy and verbose sermon.

As I opened the book I suddenly realised that it was a Bible belonging to the church.

I opened it at random and I began to read from Isaiah chapter 53. I knew little Scripture but I remembered my grandfather once preaching from this chapter. He said it referred only to the suffering servant Israel and was nothing to do with Jesus. I wondered, as I read the chapter, whether or not he was wrong. Maybe this was about the

Messiah. The Christians claimed that Jesus was the Messiah. They said He was the Holy One of Israel. He, they believed, was their Messiah, their Christ. They said that Yeshua fulfilled all the Old Testament Scriptures.

'Who has believed our message?' verse one asked. I did not believe, but wanted to so very much now.

I read on further until I had read the whole chapter. Then I began to read it over again and homed in on the third verse.

"He was despised and rejected by men."

I had both despised Him and rejected Him.

"Lord Yeshua, come into my life," I prayed inwardly, closing my eyes as tightly as I could.

It was then, having opened my eyes, that I saw clearly outlined the head and shoulders of a very bright Being. I suppose it was all over in a few seconds but, during that time, oblivious of the large congregation, I put out my hand to touch Him. The One who created the beautiful pink rose I once picked from the Convent's garden was there before me.

I had secretly sought after God. Now my search had been rewarded. At 7.22 p.m. on 22nd August, 1962, I moved from uncertainty to faith, from darkness to light. I knew that whatever sins I had committed were forgiven. The inward peace I felt was beyond description, but nevertheless very real.

The inward yearning for God, which was a secret part of my life for about three years, was now satisfied. As I personally thanked God for my newly found salvation, the minister announced the last hymn:-

I heard the voice of Jesus say,
"Come unto me and rest;
Lay down, thou weary one, lay down
Thy head upon my breast."
I came to Jesus as I was,
Weary and worn and sad.
I found in Him my resting place
And He has made me glad.

I heard the voice of Jesus say,
"Behold I freely give
The living water - thirsty one,
Stoop down, and drink and live."
I came to Jesus and I drank
Of that life-giving stream:
My thirst was quenched, my soul revived
And now I live in Him.

I heard the voice of Jesus say,
"I am this dark world's Light.
Look unto me; thy morn shall rise,
And all thy day be bright."
I looked to Jesus and I found
In Him my Star, my Sun;
And in that light of life I'll walk
Till travelling days are done.

How apt!

3

THE RENT GARMENTS
(1963-1964)

I could not get to enough Christian meetings and services. They were no longer boring! I could not read the Bible enough. It was exciting and I was hungry for the Word of God. It seemed natural to pray to the God who loved me so much - to my Heavenly Father who called me to belong to His family. Fellowship was precious for it was a meeting together with kindred spirits. I loved it all.

I was only just tolerated by my family. They hoped beyond hope that it would be a 'nine day wonder' and I would get over it; a bit like all my other short-lived interests, such as 'Flower Power' and the C.N.D. Movement.

However, the real crunch came a year later in 1963, three months before my seventeenth birthday. I read in the Bible about the baptism of the Ethiopian eunuch. I decided then that I would be baptised, too. The minister of Bethel Evangelical Church suggested that I contact a local Baptist minister in Wimbledon who, after hearing my story, agreed to baptise me in his church.

"Don't do it, honey," begged my tearful Auntie Mary. "Your parents will be more than heartbroken."

I took no notice of my aunt's request and told my parents that I was going to be baptised one Sunday evening during the half term vacation in February.

"If you go ahead with baptism then you cannot be our

daughter any more, do you understand?" said my mother, angrily.

"I must do this thing in obedience to Hasham, Mum," I replied firmly.

She was very concerned as to how they were going to hold their heads up in the Jewish community in which we lived. "What will the neighbours say?" she asked my father.

"Never mind the damn neighbours, what will this do for my new business? Who will buy from the father of a Jesus worshipper?" asked my dad, shaking his head and looking worried.

"Our people will cross the street rather than speak to the family of a girl who has shamed her parents in the sight of Hasham and Israel," interjected the old Rabbi, my grand-father, waving his arms about furiously.

They shrank from the shame; understandably so. It is always a disgraceful thing for a Jewish family to lose a member in this way. How I wished they realised that becoming a Messianic believer was not a denial of one's Jewishness, but a fulfilment of the whole thing.

On a cold Sunday evening in February, dressed in thick, warm, winter clothing, I took my big colourful bath towel and walked along to the little Baptist Chapel to be baptised by immersion.

During the baptismal service I sat in the front pew with a deacon's wife. As we sang the first hymn I slowly turned my head. My eyes swept the congregation to see if my friends from Bethel Evangelical Church were there to support me and witness my baptism as they had promised. Not one came. My eyes filled with tears. I gripped the end of the pew to steady myself as if to keep hold of my faith somehow.

45

"No one," I murmured to the deacon's wife, my voice sounding strangely husky. "I've got no one," and again, as though it were someone else who spoke, "Me ... I have no friends and now I'll have no family."

The hymn finished and we sat down together. Where was the joy I expected?

"Shh ... don't let the enemy, the devil, get to you, dear," she said, gently, as she gripped my hand.

"What does she know?" I thought to myself. "She's not Jewish."

The Baptist minister was at the front of the church and was making his way slowly down the steps into the pool of water. He came back into focus as I blinked away the blinding tears. He smiled and beckoned to me.

I was wearing a purpose-made, long, white gown with weights in the hem. To doubly ensure the gown did not billow up in the water there were four strings which tied around my feet. They were a little too tight, but there was no time to loosen them.

I walked forward and down into the pool. The minister held me, pushed me back under the water and raised me up again, proclaiming, "I baptise thee... in the Name of the Father, Son and Holy Spirit..."

After the service the minister asked one of the church members if she would give me a lift home in her car. She agreed. It was not out of her way for she lived reasonably near us.

"Will you be alright?" she asked as she pulled up outside the huge, wrought iron gates through which we could see our house silhouetted strongly against the dark, wintry night sky.

I nodded, and walked carefully along the long drive. A

large dog barked loudly and startled me.

"Who's there?" shouted a man's voice.

"It's okay, Jake, it's only me," I called to the gardener-cum-caretaker.

"Sorry, Miss," he said, half blinding me by shining his torch in my face. "Oi didn't know it were you. You been out, 'ave you then, Miss? It ain't no night for a young lady out alone, if you pardon me saying so."

He pulled his German Shepherd dog back and told it to 'shut up'.

I went to the front door and, by a light that was shining brightly in the large porch, looked in my handbag for my house key. It was not there. I felt in my pocket. It was not in there either. In my haste to get to the baptismal service I had forgotten it. I had previously planned to sneak in through the front door and go straight up the stairs to my own room, but with no key that was impossible.

"Oh, well," I thought, as I rang the doorbell, "Here goes!" I felt more than a little apprehensive. How would my family receive me? What would they say? What would they do?

My Auntie Mary, who was one of the guests staying with us for a couple of weeks, opened the door. She gasped when she saw me, just as if she had seen a ghost. As I went to walk in she stood in my way.

"Hey, Auntie, I do live here, you know!" I said.

"Becky is here!" she called in a fairly loud and agitated voice to my parents.

"Who?" asked my dad, making an appearance. "Who? I know no one of that name," he claimed and turned his face away.

I pushed my way passed my aunt and told my father not

to say such silly things. My mother and cousin Sam walked into the large hall and stared at me. Grandfather was pushed in his wheelchair by a nurse. The old man looked sternly at me. He then put his head in his hands and wept bitterly.

Sam covered his mouth and giggled at me. Someone smacked his ear and he disappeared into another room in tears. Dad and Mother looked angry, Auntie Mary disappointed. Then it happened. The four, all as one, rent their garments there in front of me, denoting that they severed all connections with me.

"No! Stop it!" I screamed at them. "Please stop it! I do not deserve this. You can't do this to me!"

It was of no use. One after the other told me to get out. I begged them to let me stay the night and then I would go in the morning. They refused.

"Where do I go at this time of night?" I asked.

"That's your problem," said Dad, his face white with rage.

"You should have thought of that before getting baptised," said Auntie Mary.

"Go on, get out, Jesus worshipper, and see if your Jesus will take care of you. Go on, get out!" yelled my mother hysterically, tears running down her face.

"You've brought shame upon Israel," wept my grandpa', choking on his words. He went into an adjoining room and I could hear his loud sobs. What grief I caused the dear old man.

I left the warmth of the large family house and walked out into the cold night air and back along the drive in the direction of the wrought iron gates. The dog barked again when he heard my footsteps.

"You ain't going out again? Bit late, ain't it, Miss?" commented Jake.

I was too choked up to reply.

Before going through the gates and on to the street, I turned and looked back at the big old house which had been my home for seventeen years. The front door slammed shut and was securely locked behind me. My whole body began to shake both from the cold and from being so upset. I cried, my face pushed hard against the wrought iron.

Once through the gates, I felt very scared to be alone on the dark South London street where anything could have happened to me. I ran to a red telephone box. Mercifully, it was in working order and had not been vandalised. I telephoned Directory Enquiries and found out the telephone number of the Science Mistress who originally had taken me to Bethel Evangelical Church.

"Oh, I thank God you are in," I said, when she answered the telephone. "Please, please help me. I am really frightened."

She instructed me to stay where I was and she would drive to fetch me. After what seemed about twenty very long minutes, her small, shiny black saloon car drove up to where I was standing. I was so glad to see it.

"Whatever are your parents thinking of, girl? You are not quite seventeen. You are still a schoolgirl," she said to me when we were sipping hot cocoa in her home. "They can't turn out an under-age girl."

It was hard for a non-Jew to comprehend the situation.

"I missed you at the baptism," I said, looking disappointed. "I felt rejected by you, too. I wish you'd been there, you know." I continued, "I had no one who I really knew at the service."

She did not attempt to justify herself. Nevertheless, she obviously sensed my added hurt.

It was still the school holidays, but I knew that Reverend Mother, who was the headmistress, would be at the School. I telephoned her from my friend's home and explained about the rift with my family.

"Your grandfather has paid the School Fees up until the end of the term; you know, until we break up for the Easter holidays ..." she informed me.

"So I can return to school?" I interrupted.

"Well, it's not really a good idea. You see, you are a weekly boarder and we cannot be responsible for you at weekends or if you are ill. I honestly think that, in the light of what has happened, you would be better staying away. I'll have a chat with your grandfather," she said, "but I think it will be hopeless. He isn't an easy man at the best of times, is he?"

I put down the receiver. What would I do about completing my education? What about my exams? I could go to evening classes, but it would not be the same for me. I considered how I would miss school life.

The teacher friend, who kindly took me in, made it clear that my stay could only be a temporary arrangement. Her apartment was very small and I was having to sleep on her sofa at night.

I needed to find a place of my own, but that cost money - something I did not have! I decided to look for a job and then accommodation.

I went to an employment agency where I was told that a large London bookshop wanted an assistant. I applied and they accepted me. I worked there for eleven months - eleven pay cheques!

One Sunday, when I was at Bethel Evangelical Church, the minister's wife took me aside.

"How are you?" she asked, putting her arm around me.

"I am fine!" I replied.

"Have you been in touch with your family?" she enquired.

"I have tried to contact them. I telephoned them, but, when they knew it was me, well ... they put the receiver down. I have written, but they have not replied. As far as they are concerned I do not exist. They will not have me back."

She asked me if I had been successful in finding alternative accommodation. I shook my head.

"That's what we thought. My husband and I have decided that you should come and live with us. Now, don't protest! We have plenty of room. Since Joy and Ruth have married and left home, well, we just rattle around in our big, old house. It will be nice for us to have you as part of our family. We really do want you. Okay?" she said, giving me a hug.

I was warmly accepted into the bosom of their family and I was just about as happy as I could possibly be. I loved them dearly and they, in turn, showed me what it was like to be really loved and wanted. Family life with them was precious and I thank God for it.

I was happy, not only with the minister and his wife, but with my job in the bookshop, Nevertheless, I wanted to both further my education and to seriously embark upon a career. Therefore, in September 1964, I decided to train to become a Registered General Nurse at a well known London teaching hospital.

4

OH, NURSE!
(1964-1967)

My initiation into nursing must have made many a hospital farce appear somewhat mundane. A Roman Catholic Nurse Tutor said she was praying to St. Jude, the supposed saint of hopeless cases, for me!

Having completed the obligatory three months in the Preliminary Training School, I was 'let loose' upon the unsuspecting patients of the men's surgical ward.

"Nurse."

Nothing.

"NURSE!"

I suddenly realised that the Sister was calling me. I stood up very straight, smoothed down my crisp new uniform and nervously bustled over to where she was standing.

"When I call you, Nurse, you do not keep me waiting. Do you understand?" she boomed.

"Yes, Ma'am." I said in a less confident tone, lowering my eyes.

"Mr. Morgan has been very ill and has to stay on 'bed rest'. He needs the toilet. See to him!" she ordered.

"Yes, Ma'am," I said in an even less confident tone.

I promptly went to a Mr. Wood's bedside and greeted him as 'Mr. Morgan'.

"I ain't him. You want old Bert. He's there in that bed.

There!" Mr. Wood said, pointing to Mr. Morgan's bed.

Mr. Morgan was looking very agitated. "I want the commode, Miss," he said.

I did not know what to do because the Sister stressed that he had been very ill and needed to remain on 'bed rest'. What was I to do with this patient who wanted the commode and who could not leave his bed? A couple of minutes later I had solved the problem. Mr. Morgan was perched on the commode, which I had placed on the bed.

When the Sister came to see how I was coping she was aghast to see the head of a terrified Mr. Morgan peering at her from above the screens around his bed!

After that stint, the same very strict Sister asked me if I really thought that I was cut out for nursing! When I told her that I was going to continue with my training she appeared alarmed and quickly warned the Sister of the medical ward where I was to work next.

My academic ability in the classroom of the School of Nursing was good, but, when on the wards, I did not seem to have very much practical common sense!

Putting me in the Operating Theatre during the latter half of my first year of nurse training was a real mistake by the administrators. Almost the worst thing I did was to drop a large, heavy metal instrument which fell with a thud on the big toe of the Consultant Gynaecologist. After that I was relegated to cleaning metal instruments or counting swabs!

Back on the wards, my reputation had gone before me!

"That patient is going for a tonsillectomy later today, Nurse," stated a mischievous, newly qualified Staff Nurse to gullible me. "Did you know that there are tiny hairs on the tonsils?"

"No," I replied, looking blank.

"Well," she said, "You'll have to shave them off. Okay?"

"Yes, Staff Nurse," I replied, and quickly went to get an open razor from the clinic room! I was stopped by her just in time - before I did untold damage!

During my second and third years of nurse training, the Roman Catholic Nurse Tutor was convinced that St. Jude must have been listening to her and watching over me as she pleaded on her knees for the safety of the hospital's patients! You see, I became quite a good nurse, even though I say it myself, and succeeded in being awarded a silver medal on completion of my training. My ward reports during the first year apparently prevented the acquisition of the gold medal!

The medal was presented in London by Her Royal Highness Princess Alexandra. All of the nurses at the prize-giving ceremony were groomed to look exceptionally smart. We even wore white gloves so that we did not transmit germs to the royal hand when it was shaken! For such an important occasion, it was decided by the Hospital's executive Matron that those involved with prize-giving should be taught to march in order to impress the Princess.

"Right turn!" shouted the physical training instructor in my ear.

I often used to find it a problem distinguishing my left from my right and invariably ended up almost facing the person behind me, which made us all, with the exception of the physical training instructor, collapse into fits of laughter!

During most of the three years' training which preceded our prize-giving, we were made to share rooms in the Nurses' Home with the other student nurses. I was fortunate to be paired with a girl who was an evangelical

Christian. Helen was brought up by her parents to attend a Scottish Presbyterian Church, but she had only recently come to know Jesus Christ as her personal Saviour and Lord. It was a joy for us to be able, from the start, to enjoy rich Christian fellowship together.

Incidentally, Helen is now married to a delightful Christian businessman and they have three beautiful teen-age children. I visited her in their lovely home a short while ago and was surprised to discover her to be so tidy. She certainly was not when we shared a room; then, I was the tidy one. Her willingness to live in a chaotic state some-times irritated me beyond belief. Because of this we made an imaginary line in the room - her side resembled a tip and my side was kept spick and span!

One Thursday evening we arranged to have a prayer meeting in our room. We heard that one of the Sisters, who was an ex-missionary from Northern India, was planning to join us. During nurse training in the London of the 1960's everyone lived in fear of the Sisters. I certainly did, and not always without reason!

"Quick! Tidy up all your things, Helen," I said, giving her a gentle push towards her heap of untidy clothing, books and unmade bedding. "Sister Davies is joining us for the prayer meeting. Whatever will she think if she sees this mess?"

Helen responded immediately and quickly pushed her clothing into her already overfull wardrobe. The books were precariously piled up onto an overfull shelf and the ones which did not keep their balance and fell down were kicked under her bed. The bedding was pulled up and covered over with a green, creased up, old quilt - hardly hospital fashion!

At the end of the prayer meeting, Helen bounced up, plugged in the electric coffee percolator and asked, "Who's for a coffee?"

I winced when I realised that the tin of dried milk powder, bag of damp lumpy sugar, mugs and spoons were on the top shelf of a small overhead cupboard. It was too late to warn Helen who, without thinking, opened the cupboard door - the contents fell over the Sister's head, thereby knocking her white cap over one eye! Somewhat humiliated, she decided not to come again to our prayer meetings, but to find her fellowship elsewhere with quieter, more mature Christians.

Throughout our nurse training a late pass was granted to us just once a week; otherwise we were required to be in by 9.00 p.m. every evening! One night I came in quite late and was unable to sneak past the night watchman who guarded the hospital's entrance. (Grace did not always appear to abound!)

"Wot's yer name, Nurse?" he asked.

"Marie Antoinette!" I replied, cheekily.

Next morning, he reported to the Matron that Nurse Mary-Anne Twonette came in at 11.30 p.m. and she could show no late pass!

Nursing was for me, rarely without incident! Just after I qualified as a Registered Nurse I found that one of the patients who was in my care had died. An hour later, when a new student nurse and I were laying him out, I asked her, for the sake of a form which needed to be completed, his religion.

"Jewish," replied the young student nurse, nonchalantly.

"What? Oh no!" I exclaimed. "We'll have to un-lay him and quickly!" I knew that the body must not be touched until a Rabbi had said special prayers.

The dead Jew was somehow forced back into his pyjamas by the two of us and warmed up with a space blanket.

The Rabbi was then called. When he arrived, looking not unlike my late grandfather, he commented that the body was a bit stiff. We volunteered no information and I just stood there looking blank.

After the obligatory prayers were finally said over the body, the Rabbi told me that the dead Jew could then be laid out. So 'out' we laid him again!

With the body ready for its journey to the mortuary, I called for the hospital's porters who then announced that they could not get their mortuary trolley up to our ward because the elevator was out of order.

"Well, can't you simply carry the body to your mortuary trolley?" I asked the porter, impatiently.

"No, Nurse. We ain't paid to touch no dead body, are we, Sid?"

Sid shook his head.

"Well, Nurse, I suggest yer get advice from yer Matron. Don't yer fink she should, Sid?" continued the porter.

Sid showed agreement by pushing his hands into his pockets and nodding his head at an alarming rate!

I telephoned the Matron's office and was able to speak to the tyrant herself! She suggested that the two porters push their trolley around to the back where the fire escape was situated and that the young student nurse and myself should carry the body down. No patients or members of the public would be around in that vicinity to see us.

We proceeded to put the Matron's unusual plan into action. A third of the way down the spiral fire escape the air came of out of the dead Jew's lungs and we heard what was like a loud, deep sigh. The new nurse was not aware that this often happened. Her eyes widened and she screamed, letting go of the Jew! He was too heavy for me and I dropped him ... *Bump! Bumper-dee-bump! Bump-er-dee-bump!*

"Er, hello, Ma'am ... It is Nurse Jacobi here, Ma'am. Er, yes, well, it's about that Jew ... W-well, I er, um, d-don't know quite h-how to explain...," I stammered down the telephone to the Matron.

Another very unusual occasion involved a Moslem and me, of course!

A Pakistani lady died. The cause of death was 'Status Asthmaticus'. The grief-stricken family requested that her body be flown back to Pakistan. I did not know how to go about advising them and so I contacted one of London's Registrars for Births and Deaths, who said that they would have to acquire certain documents from him and a 'box' for her. When he said 'box' he meant 'coffin' - obviously!

I passed on the message to the grieving husband and father. "Okay," they replied, and promptly went on their way. About an hour-and-a-half or so, later the two men returned triumphantly carrying a giant-sized cardboard box which had previously been used to store and carry 24 packets of Kellogg's Cornflakes to the local grocery store!

The loss of a friend (1967-1968)

In the Nurses' Home I was part of a small committee which ran the Inter-Hospitals' Nurses' Christian Fellowship.

How I loved those meetings. We were a very mixed bag but we were bound together by faith in our Lord. There was a genuine Christian love amongst the fellowship and I now look back upon that time with fondness.

One of our group was a lovely Christian girl called Sophie.

One evening Helen and I were slowly trudging up the seemingly endless stone staircase to the fourth floor of the Nurses' Home where we shared a double room. We were feeling extremely tired after an exceptionally hard day's work in the busy Casualty Department of the hospital.

"Can you smell gas?" I asked Helen as we approached the fourth floor's landing.

She sniffed and agreed there was a smell of gas. It was obviously coming from the tiny kitchen area allocated for the nurses' shared use.

"Pooh! It's bad, isn't it?" I said, holding my nose. Just as we were about to investigate, there was a loud explosion.

"Oh, no! Help!" I yelled at the top of my voice. "Sophie is in there. Quickly!"

Helen and I were somehow able to enter the kitchen, smash the window for air, and then drag Sophie out into the corridor. A passing cleaner, who stopped to stare, was instructed to put out an emergency call.

"Cardiac arrest! Emergency! Move!" shouted Helen. "Go on! Move! Phone 505."

Sophie's heart had stopped and she was, in effect, dead.

Helen tried to give mouth-to-mouth resuscitation but it was difficult to maintain a clear airway, for the gas explosion had severely burnt and disfigured Sophie's beautiful face.

I was thumping on Sophie's chest, trying desperately to get her heart working again. We knew her burns needed urgent attention but the two of us were aware that the resuscitation took first priority.

Suddenly, in response to the emergency call put out by

the cleaner, there were doctors and experienced nursing staff, pushing us out of the way, and Sophie was raced to the nearby Intensive Care Unit.

We ran behind them, but, as we reached the Unit, the doors were slammed in our faces. Our dear, dear friend was in there and we were not allowed to be with her. We suddenly felt so frustrated - so helpless.

Helen, as if in a daze, sat down on a nearby chair. She was already very exhausted, and now so upset. She kept gulping to rid herself of the lump in her throat and looking up to blink the tears away.

I leaned hard against the wall. Slowly, I slid down it and sat on the floor. Tears rolled down my face.

"What if she dies...?" I began to repeat the words over and over to myself.

"Shut up!" Helen snapped at me. "Just shut up. Okay?"

Two young doctors who had been working in the Intensive Care Unit came out looking physically drained.

"Please can you tell us how our friend is?" I asked.

"Her name is Sophie Tyler," Helen added.

"I'm not at liberty to say," said one. "Sorry."

"I suppose I can tell you," said the other who was obviously more senior, "It should really be the relatives I tell first but, as you are the two who tried to save her life, I don't suppose anyone will object."

We looked at him through our tears, urging him to tell us everything. I clenched my fists by my side, my nails marking the palms of my hands.

"She took about twenty strong sleeping tablets and then put her head into the gas oven which somehow exploded. She's now on a life-support machine." he said. "Why she did it is an enigma. Her parents are on their way here now.

Perhaps they'll throw some light on her situation. Anyway, the main thing is to get her well."

We listened through the doorway to the noisy breathing sounds of the life-support machine. We carried on listening for about half-an-hour through the door ... then it stopped. There was only silence. Sophie was brain dead. All hope was gone. The respirator was switched off. It was as if the whole world had stopped and was in total silence. Totally and completely silent. Sophie was dead.

We would never see her again. How we wept! Helen and I held each other and we sobbed together until it seemed we had no more tears to shed.

The funeral service was held a few days later at the Pentecostal Chapel where Sophie's parents were active members.

I entered the large airy building and moved into a pew on the right hand side of the church. I sat down slowly and tried to say a prayer, but my mind was blank. Sitting up, I could see the shiny brown coffin, the top of which was covered with many floral wreaths. A lump came into my throat as I realised that my dear friend's body was in there.

I began to wonder if I had worked hard enough to resuscitate her. Had I failed her? My whole body began to tremble and I wanted to sob loudly. The Christian Sister, Miss Davies, who once came to our prayer meeting, was sitting in the pew just behind. She leaned forward to touch my left shoulder. The touch was meant to comfort me. I could not cope. I could not stay. I needed to get out. The first hymn was announced and I pushed past others in the pew and fled out of the church. Once outside, I faced the brick wall and cried and cried, almost choking with my grief.

After the funeral all the joy seemed to disappear from

me. Sadness overwhelmed me. I just did not know how to handle the terrible tragedy. No-one seemed to be able to provide me with any logical answers as to why God allowed her to die.

The Christian Fellowship ceased and many nurses either moved onto other situations or slipped back in their Christian ways.

It was a bad time for nearly all of us. Life was just awful without Sophie.

I decided it was time I too moved on, so, in September 1968, I embarked upon the intensive training to become a qualified midwife at the British Hospital for Mothers and Babies in Woolwich, London, where the majority of the staff there were committed Christians.

5

CALLED TO SERVE
(1969-1970)

Just over half-way through the midwifery training course, I was resting peacefully alone in my room at the Nurses' Home after assisting a woman with the delivery of her third child - a much wanted son. It was then that my mind flashed back to a time shortly after my baptism when I was asked by a friend to take her Sunday School class. She was unable to take the class for she had a very heavy cold and an extremely sore throat.

"I can't do that, Anne. I know virtually nothing about Sunday School teaching," I protested.

Anne assured me that I would not have to do much more than just sit and supervise the children.

"A missionary will be coming to talk to the children about his work overseas and he will show them some slides. Just welcome him and keep the children in order. You know, make sure they don't run riot and set the church on fire, or something! And remember to thank him at the end of his talk. That's all there is to do, Becky!" she croaked. "You'll do it for me, won't you? It's dead easy!"

I have since found that people often over-simplify things when they want you to do them a favour!

It was not quite as easy for me as she made out. I had to open in prayer, sing a hymn with the children whilst playing an old out of tune 'honky-tonk' type of piano, and introduce the speaker. I forgot the speaker's name and got away with that awkward moment by saying, "This afternoon, boys and girls, we have a missionary with us who is going to explain about his work and show us some of his coloured slides. Now, I'll leave him to introduce himself..."

I stepped back, clapping. All the children clapped, cheered or whistled - the sort of whistle where they put two fingers in their mouths and shriek out a terrible piercing sound.

"That's enough! Settle down, please!" I commanded in a loud, authoritative voice to which they, surprisingly enough, responded.

The missionary's opening slide showed a large golden cornfield and the crop was just ready to be harvested.

"Perhaps one day God might call you to be a 'harvester' for Him," he said. "There will be many souls lost to God if we don't tell them about Him."

His words shot through me like an electric current. Whether or not God spoke to any of the children in that meeting I do not know, but I became aware, for the first time in my life, of a sphere of service to which I was being called.

That night, at the age of seventeen, I knelt down by the side of my bed and told God that I would be willing to go wherever He called.

Two weeks later two friends in their late twenties, who attended Bethel Evangelical Church, told me that they were going to Herne Bay Court for a weekend's conference, run by a missionary society which operated in India. They invited me to go with them.

It was a memorable weekend for me. I learned about the opportunities in India and I developed an overwhelming compassion for those dying without Christ. The missionary society stimulated me by their literature and contact with missionaries. God confirmed to me that He was truly calling me to India and I needed to keep the goal in view.

During the following four years I sometimes found the long delay an irksome test. I wanted to go to India there and then. I did not want to wait. Many of God's choice servants have had to learn the hard lesson of patience before they could be used, and so had I! The years of training and waiting were an extremely valuable time for learning the lesson that patience is one of the essential qualities required in the life, work and trials of the overseas missionary worker.

The waiting years gave me time to both test and learn about the call itself. I studied the biographies of those, missionaries in particular, who followed the path wholly appointed by God. When I read about the simple but definite call to Abraham where God said, 'Get thee out of thy country ... unto a land that I will show thee' (Genesis 12:1), I foolishly thought that my call would take the same form! I honestly thought in my naivety that a loud voice, which only I could hear, would bellow from the heavens saying, "Get thee out of England ... unto a land called India!" Not so!

Nevertheless, God was clearly speaking to me about overseas missionary work and I had to obey. I was being guided along a particular path which was leading to that vast continent of India with its teeming millions of 'lost' people. All I had to do was to walk in His way. I learnt that He would only reveal the path to me if I was willing to forsake the wrongs in my life which grieved Him. It was then that I would know with assurance the right way.

Like Isaiah of old I developed an overwhelming conviction of unworthiness for the task, but I knew God's forgiveness and was willing to respond to the challenge, "Whom shall I send, and who will go for us?" with the reply, "Here am I, send me!" (Isaiah 6:8).

God brought to my remembrance the words, "You have not chosen me but I have chosen you" (John 15:16).

It was then, at the age of twenty three, with my nursing and midwifery training behind me, that I responded in a positive way to His call by applying to a Women's Missionary Training College situated in a fairly pleasant suburb of West London.

Training college (1969)

Having been accepted as a student there in the October of 1969 I naively thought that, in the almost perfect setting of such a missionary training college, it would be much easier to live a holy and dedicated life, but it did not quite work out like that. I took myself with me and all the others brought themselves, too!

There was a very serious person called Rachel, who voiced the opinion that my sense of fun was beneath her and probably 'of the devil'! I thought she was too good to be true. We found it very difficult to get on together even though we both tried so hard.

Then there was a noisy, giggly student called Sarah who knitted a lot. Oh, the clacking of those needles! Worse still, when she used the wash-basin, or the bath, she simply pulled out the plug and walked away, leaving it for the next person to clean. If Rachel annoyed me, Sarah really made my blood boil.

More irksome still, if one is irritated by certain things in a missionary training college, the phrase 'G.M.T.' is top of the list. It is commonly used in certain missionary circles and stands for 'Good Missionary Training'. It is generally said in a jolly fashion when someone is called upon to do something particularly horrid, such as eating salty, lukewarm porridge topped with prunes. It was said to me on many occasions and I felt, at times, that my chances of becoming a good missionary were slim!

It is probably never easy for those in their mid-twenties, who have already earned their place as adults in a secular sphere, to come again under authority in such a college.

During the first week of college we were required to pay our fees.

"Please line up outside my office, ladies, and I will relieve you of your fees for this term!" said the Secretary, clapping her hands to gain our attention. I lingered to the back of the line. Emma, who stood directly in front of me, took a chequebook from her handbag and turned to me.

"Have you a pen that I could borrow, please? I have left mine in my room. I'm not very well organised yet!"

"Yes, sure, a pen is about all I do have," I laughed.

"What do you mean?" Emma quizzed.

I explained that I had been praying the Lord would provide my fees.

"Now here I am, as poor as a church mouse! I believe that I am meant to be here ..."

"Well, then, if you are meant to be here, God will provide," interrupted Emma, "Just have faith!"

Eventually, all the students had paid their fees and I alone was left.

"Er, my name is Rebecca Jacobi. I believe God has

called me to this college and I have prayed He would provide my fees. However, all I have is one meagre note in my purse and it is not worth much," I said in a flurry of words.

"Hey, stop talking, Rebecca, and let me explain," the Secretary laughed. "Your fees for the whole year have already been paid. We have an allowance to hand over to you so that your personal needs can be met. Books will be very expensive and the money for purchasing the necessary literature is here for you. In fact, any expenses you incur during your time with us will be met."

"But ... who? Who has given all this money?" I asked.

"Sorry, dear, I'm not at liberty to say. The Christian wishes to remain anonymous. Now, I suggest you close your mouth and go to your room!"

I never did discover who paid my expenses during my time at College, but I thanked God for them. God is faithful - He provided my needs through the generosity of His obedient servant. My wants were never, thankfully, given to me in case I became puffed up with the materialism of this world.

During the hot summer of 1970, after surviving my first year at missionary training college, I was roped in to help at a beach mission. It was organised by the Children's Special Service Mission (C.S.S.M.).

"C.S.S.M. can also mean 'come single, soon married', Becky, so watch out! There might be a man about!" joked a friend from college.

Bill (1970)

It was at the beach mission that I met a handsome, young theological student called Bill. I liked him immediately.

On the last day of the mission Bill walked up to where

I was sitting. He sat down on the bench beside me, took hold of my hand and asked if he could see me again. We had only known each other for a couple of weeks, but I secretly hoped that our friendship would continue.

Back in college, I confided in my friend Jilly concerning my feelings for Bill.

"Our chemistry just seemed to mix ..." I began.

"Chemistry? Rot! In my experience it has always made nitro-glycerine!" interrupted Jilly.

"Well, we are going to see each other again," I said.

"You hope you will!" she laughed.

"What do you mean?" I asked, following her into the bathroom. "I am over 21 - I can do as I please."

I sat on the edge of the empty bath while she filled the basin, ready to wash her hair. She pushed me aside in order to reach for her towel and reminded me that I would need the Principal's permission to sit next to the young man in church, let alone go out with him on a date.

I got up from the edge of the bath and stormed out, banging the door after me.

"Petty, stupid rules! I'm not a child." I shouted.

"G.M.T.!" yelled my companion, which irritated me even more.

The Principal did give me permission and I went to a church service with Bill. Various dates followed and we became very fond of each other indeed.

One Saturday afternoon Bill telephoned me at the college. Another student answered the telephone and called for me. "Becky, it's the man himself!" she smiled, holding out the telephone receiver.

I grabbed it from her. Oh, it was him! I could feel my heart beating quickly and, when I tried to speak, I was so breathless, just as if I had run a mile. I was reacting like a silly young heroine in a cheap romantic novel! He told me that he was going to call for me the next day. I could hardly wait. The time seemed to drag.

The following day, Bill and I set out for the magnificent Surrey countryside. Reaching our destination, we sat for what seemed quite a while looking at the panoramic view. The sun was making an effort to come out, but really not succeeding very well. We got out of the car.

Bill put his arm around me.

"Cold?" he asked.

"No, not really," I replied.

"Happy?"

"Something like that," I laughed.

"I want to ask you something - just to reassure myself," he said enigmatically.

"What is it?"

"It is true for you, isn't it? This overwhelming feeling that we have for each other - it is as true for you as it is for me, isn't it?" he asked softly.

"Yes, it's true," I whispered.

We must have stayed together for a long time, walking, holding hands, enjoying each other's company. When we returned the borrowed car to its garage it was getting dark. I remember feeling as though I was on the edge of a precipice. I think Bill felt that too. We said how desperately we loved each other.

Bill said that he had to leave the keys of the car in his friend's apartment and suggested I come up with him. I refused rather too vehemently. Bill reminded me that his friend was not coming back until late, but I still refused.

"I am going back to the college. I really must go back.

I'll catch a train," my voice quaked nervously.

"It's raining. You have no umbrella and you'll get soaked. You mustn't catch a cold - that will never do. Do sit down, darling. I want to be with you," he said.

"We'd both be very, very foolish. Bill, I can't stay, you know, really I can't."

"Just a little while," he pleaded.

I stood my ground. "No, no, I must go. I have enough money. I will get a taxi back to college. It is still raining, but not very much," I replied.

"I should really see you back to the college - not leave you here to get yourself back," he said.

"It doesn't matter, really it doesn't," I insisted.

He tried again to persuade me to stay a little longer, but I had called a cab. Bill blew a kiss as I climbed into the back of the taxi.

In the car I managed to get myself under control and it gave me a little time to think. If I had allowed it Bill would have come on too strong, and it worried me. He said that loving each other was all that really mattered. To me it was not all that mattered.

I could not become cheap and low. Self respect mattered, and decency. He had told me that he loved me and that he would love me until the end of his life. Yet if he behaved in a way that the world expected, then I knew that this would be the beginning of the end - not the end of our loving each other, but the end of our being together. There could be no sordidness in our relationship. It had to be open before the Lord. Jesus must come first.

The next day I received a telephone call from Bill.

"This will have to be the end of our relationship unless God comes first. I know what I feel about yesterday evening.

I know about the strain of our different lives - our lives apart from each other. The feeling of guilt and doing wrong is too strong, isn't it? It is too great a price to pay for the happiness we could have together," I stated firmly to him.

"I know all this because it is the same for me, too. We must be very careful. We can't do such violence to our hearts and lives," he agreed.

"Ah, well, I am so glad that we have cleared up that matter," I said with a sigh.

"Can I see you again soon?" he asked - a sense of urgency was in his voice.

"No, not yet. I have a lot of work to catch up on at college. I must not neglect my studies. I am sure it is the same for you," I added.

There was a silence on the telephone and I wondered if he was still there. He was. "I want you to promise me something, Rebecca," he continued.

"What is it?" I asked.

"That you'll meet me next Thursday," he said.

"Where?" I weakened in my resolve.

"At Victoria Station at 5.30 p.m. On platform 5," he suggested.

"Alright," I said.

"I have something for you. Something very special. I really must see you. You really will come, won't you?" he persisted.

"Yes, I'll come," I sighed.

I met him outside platform 5 at 5.30 p.m. as I had promised. It was hardly credible that we had known each other for so short a time. It had gone by so quickly.

"Are you all right, darling?" he asked, holding me a little too close.

I nodded and he kissed me several times. I felt uncomfortable as we were in a public place.

"Becky, I love you very much and I have something for you. I hope it fits!" he said, reaching into his jacket pocket for a small jewel box. "It was my grandmother's."

"Oh, it's beautiful!" I exclaimed, as he slipped the diamond engagement ring onto the third finger of my left hand.

"Marry me," he whispered into my ear.

I nodded.

Back in college, I flashed my ring under the noses of all my friends before making my way to the Principal's study where she gave me her blessing. I was so happy.

Wedding plans were put into action. We were to be married at the end of my final term.

One Saturday afternoon a more mature friend, called Jessica, came with me to choose my wedding dress. We went to a smart bridal boutique situated in London's West End. There I tried on the most beautiful dresses. One dress in particular looked absolutely wonderful and fitted me like a glove. The assistant asked me when the wedding would take place.

"Oh, when I've finished at college," I replied in a casual way.

"She's going to be a minister's wife," said my friend. Her words went suddenly through me like an electric shock - a minister's wife!

"I think I'll leave purchasing the dress for now," I said, unzipping the magnificent fairytale gown as quickly as I could. "It's a bit too pricy for me."

Jessica and I left the boutique and went for a cup of expresso coffee and a slice of gateau in a nearby cafe.

"What was all that about?" she enquired in a whisper, leaning forward on her elbows towards me.

"I need to talk to Bill," I replied. "I am so confused just now."

The next day I met Bill for the morning church service at Westminster Chapel. A picnic lunch followed in St. James' Park, London.

"Bill, what are you called by God to do after college?" I asked. "We need to discuss our future, don't we?"

"I'm going to be a famous minister of a big Baptist church and you, Becky, will be my lovely wife!" he replied with annoying flippancy. He squeezed my hand and gave me a peck on the side of my face.

"Oh, please stop it and be serious, won't you?" I snapped.

I felt my heart beating quickly within me. I stiffened and looked away.

"Becky, whatever is the matter?" he asked, hugging me close to his chest.

I pulled away, slipped the ring off my finger and handed it back to him.

"What? What are you doing? That's your ring. We are engaged to be married, darling," exclaimed Bill.

"Bill, I cannot be your wife," I began, trying to fight back the tears which were running down my face. "God has, you say, apparently called you to the Baptist ministry here in England and God is clearly calling me to the mission field ... in India. I cannot marry you for I would be stepping out of God's will if I remained in England. Oh, Bill ... Bill, it has just been a fantasy - a dream - we're not meant for each other - we're poles apart."

"Look," he sternly protested, "You can be used just as

much here for the Lord as my wife, can't you, girl?"

His sudden outburst worried me - I had not seen that side of him before. He was not prepared to discuss our situation - he made it clear that he wanted everything his way.

"Please, drive me back to the college," I said firmly. "There's no point in trying to talk things over, is there?"

We drove back in complete silence. The atmosphere was uneasy to say the least. That day was our last day together. Our very last together in all our lives.

Back in the college, I walked slowly towards my room. My room mates were all out at various Bible classes. However, the Principal caught sight of me through the half-opened door of her sitting room.

"Hello," she called. "Are you alright, dear?"

"Can I talk with you, please?" I asked, half putting my head around her door. I entered gingerly into her sitting room. We sat together on a large comfortable settee and I told her my story.

"Becky, dear, I have been most concerned about this relationship in the last couple of days. At first I was delighted for you and wanted to share your joy," said the Principal, her sheer Christian love shining through.

I was confused and asked her just what she meant.

"I am relieved that you have been the one to end the relationship. I would have hated him to have rejected you. You have experienced enough trauma in your life already - I refer to your family. I heard from a cousin of mine, who is the Senior Tutor at the Theological College where Bill is a student, that Bill has been 'two-timing' you. He has been seeing his old girlfriend regularly as well as you. Dear, I am so sorry. He is just an opportunist."

I looked horrified. I could hardly believe what I was hearing. She must be mistaken.

"He has treated you very badly and has brought disgrace to the reputation of his college. Worst of all, he has brought dishonour to the name of the Lord. Oh, Rebecca, Rebecca, I wonder if he ever intended to marry you. He gave the other girl a ring, too - taken from his mother's jewel-box! I think he will be severely disciplined by the Principal and may be suspended from his college. You, Rebecca, are special to God. Man may fail you, but God will never fail. Don't you ever forget that, Okay?"

Depression

The days that followed were dark days. I was having a struggle to be my normal, cheery self and to keep up an act was not only impossible, but dishonest.

Six of us shared one large bedroom in the college and it was difficult for me to obtain the isolation I so desired.

I felt foolish to have fallen for a relationship full of injustice and dishonesty. How could I ever love or care for anyone again? How could I trust another man? How could I forgive Bill?

"I have made a hopeless mess," I told my tutor.

"No, dear, you haven't. Bill has made a mess of things - and even he isn't hopeless, is he? Not in God's sight, anyway," she replied.

"He has made a fool of me and left a miserable emptiness..." I began.

"... And a longing for revenge?" she interrupted. "But Jesus changes our attitudes to external situations. I know from my own experiences. Believe me, I really do understand. I have been there."

I wanted to go around with a bag over my head, as it were! I wanted to withdraw from everyone and everything. I was no fun to be with. I wanted to stop my world and get off. Night brought little relief. Sleep came, but so did wakefulness in the early hours. I fell into a deep sleep when it was time to get up.

"Why don't you take a short leave of absence before this depression of yours gets completely out of hand. Go away somewhere and get some rest," suggested the tutor a week or so later.

I was annoyed when I was told by her that I was depressed. Sure, I was not myself, but the show had to go on.

"If you were physically ill you wouldn't object to time off. You wouldn't feel angry if it were a *physical* illness. Why are you so angry when I say that you are emotionally sick?" reasoned the tutor.

I went to stay with the minister and his wife who kindly took me into their home when I was made homeless by my Jewish family.

"You need rest and we are going to see that you get it. You are to do nothing but laze around!" commanded the minister, "I know what I am talking about. Rest and recovery restores one's balance."

"I can't laze around. It will be too hard on your wife. She needs help with cooking and housework," I protested.

"I heard that!" called the minister's wife from the kitchen. "I can manage and I don't want you anywhere near my vacuum cleaner! You're here to rest."

Less than obedient, I helped as much as possible with the cooking!

One afternoon I went to my room. I felt so tired. The

turmoil had absorbed a lot of emotional energy and left me with sheer fatigue. The central heating was on, but the room seemed to become icy cold and dark. I was conscious of a presence - a real sense of evil. I went to stand, but I was knocked off my feet. We talk so much about the power of God, but underestimate the forces of darkness; it was these forces which were putting my soul into intense agony. I called out for God in a loud voice.

The minister's wife heard me shout and thought I was calling for her. She fled into my room, and, on seeing me, threw her arms about me and rocked me backwards and forwards.

"You have the support of Christians, you know. We love you. We are fellow travellers and we'll spur you on in understanding and faith," she said.

She wrestled in prayer with me until I knew a great peace, and we rested in the love which comes from God alone.

It was time to return to college, but I was embarrassed - too embarrassed to face the staff and the students again. The former had seen me as a tearful wreck and I thought that they would despise my weakness.

"You go back to college, dear, and hold your head up high. You've done nothing wrong," urged the minister.

Attitudes (1970 - 1971)

I returned to the Missionary Training College one Monday, well able to cope, but still just a fraction fragile.

I felt the warm glow of God's family at college. There really were those who truly cared. There were also those who tried to protect me from any conversations about marriage or singleness and I had to make it clear to them that I lived in a real world and I could not be wrapped in cotton wool, as it were!

At college we had regular guest speakers. Many of them came to tell us about their work and to ask us if we felt a call to go out with their particular mission. Others came who told us about the various problems that a missionary might encounter overseas. One day an eminent minister came who was to speak to us about 'the single lady missionary'.

"You don't have to attend, Rebecca, if you do not want to. In your case I shall understand," explained my tutor.

"Really, I am fine. I am not the first person to experience a broken engagement and I shall not be the last! I am Okay. I want to hear what this man has to say on the subject. After all, it looks as if I am going to be a single lady missionary, doesn't it?" I replied with a smile.

The speaker was very good and I enjoyed listening to everything he said. I found parts of his talk particularly thought provoking. An example of this was when he stated that, once a single lady missionary reached thirty years of age, she was unlikely to marry and she needed to come to terms with being single. He said that, if singleness was God's will for the lady missionary, then the Lord would be a husband to her.

At the end of his lecture he asked if we wanted to ask any questions.

I shot up my hand and, as I did so, I caught sight of my tutor wincing! She obviously thought that I was going to verbally slay the speaker!

"I have a question, sir," I said. "May I ask why nothing is said about the problems of the single male missionary - always only about the single lady missionary? After all, we read in Genesis 2:18, that the Lord God said, 'It is not good for *man* to live alone. I will make a suitable companion to help him'. It was the single man called Adam who needed the woman - and not the other way around! I know that we also read about virgins and widows, but we do not read about 'frustrated old spinsters'. In our society we regard single men as 'eligible bachelors', but women as 'old spinsters'. Missions regard single male missionaries as 'available for the Lord's work', and single ladies as something else. Can you answer me, sir?"

The tutor put her head in her hands. The other students turned their heads towards me and smiled. Some clapped. The speaker did not give me a satisfactory answer, but suggested that I talk to him afterwards. I had obviously put him on the spot! I was not being difficult - I really wanted an answer to these things.

I was settling down to realities and everything in my life was falling into place. Instead of looking at my own difficulties and becoming bitter and twisted, I could now honestly count my blessings. So much, I discovered, turned on my attitude. Single people, in particular, can sometimes be treated as if they are life's failures because they are unmarried. I learned, though, that, if we belong to the King of kings, then we cannot be regarded as a failure.

Unfulfilment, of whatever character, is a thorn in the flesh, valueless, useless and destructive until accepted and grafted into one's experience in a way that would result in some new growth. All of this I made a real matter of prayer and I discovered that God's grace was truly sufficient for me at that time.

When my friends Margaret and Peter made their wedding plans I was genuinely able to enter into their happiness. I did not want to remain a 'spinster of the parish' all my days. Sure, I wanted to be married and have children. After all, I was not made of stone! I was very human with very natural sexual and maternal instincts, but I knew that God was preparing the best wine for me.

College eventually came to an end in the July of 1971. I was sad to leave it and all my dear friends from there. Bill had become only a faded memory. I was on top mentally, physically and spiritually. I knew that it was the right time to apply to a particular faith mission which operated in India.

6

OVERLAND TO INDIA
(1971)

Most overseas missionary recruits usually sail or fly to their destination. However, I heard about a lady missionary who, in order to save on expenses, travelled overland to India. So, with her 'adventure' buzzing around in my mind, I spoke to those in authority at the Mission's home base, who had accepted me as a recruit, and asked their permission to do the same.

Surprisingly, they agreed to my request! Nowadays, this kind of overland trip is too difficult to even contemplate as many of the countries are either closed to Westerners or have become dangerous territories, but in the 1960's and 1970's there was little unrest and trips of this kind were often made, especially by the hippie community.

Six Australian men who had fulfilled their ambition to see much of Europe, and especially the United Kingdom, were planning to return home overland from York and there was room for one more on the trip. I saw their advertisement in the personal column of the *Daily Telegraph* and, through a letter, I applied. In my letter I did not make it clear to them that I was a woman, for I felt that I would be turned down out of hand. Imagine their surprise when we actually met in Stillington, near York!

When they saw me they shook their heads and told me it was impossible for them to accept me, for one young woman with six men could prove a problem!

"We can't consider you for the trip. We're men and, well, you are ... um ... a ..."

"Woman?" I said, completing his sentence for him.

"Yeah," he replied, winking in the direction of the other five men who were all laughing together about my application. I felt myself flush with embarrassment.

"Please, please let me come on the trip. I want to get to India. I am going to be a missionary there," I said. "I am a qualified nurse."

"A missionary, eh? Heck, I have never met a real live missionary before!" continued the spokesman with a grin.

"Well, I don't know. I don't like 'holy Joes'. Anyway, we would be sleeping mostly in third-rate hotels, or under canvas in our own little tents," interjected another.

"Please, I won't be any trouble," I pleaded. "Let me come with you."

"What do ya' think fellas, shall we give it a go? After all, a nurse could certainly prove very useful to us on our trip," asked the spokesman, turning to look at the other men for their reactions.

"She can mop my fevered brow any time," laughed one other man.

"Don't be so stupid!" I retorted, angrily.

With that, they decided to 'give it a go' and promised me faithfully to be totally honourable.

Having been accepted by the men, I decided it was best to find out the problems before they found me. Travelling through so many countries, one after the other, raises all sorts of questions in one's mind, financial not least. I was not in employment as such - I was 'owned' by the Mission and really living by faith.

I went along to a bank in the West End of London and spoke with the manager; a smart, middle-aged man, dressed in a pin-striped suit and highly polished black shoes.

"Iraq and Iran insist that I have a minimum of £100 in the bank all the time that I travel through their countries," I said.

I watched his facial expression, for £100 in the 1960's and 1970's was probably the equivalent of his monthly take-home pay! However, he agreed to allow me the sum of money.

"Just thinking of awful emergencies ... what if I need the £100? How easy is it for you to get the money out to me?" I asked.

"You've got our telephone number. I know your voice and so do some of my staff now. Just say 'Shalom' and your mother's maiden name when you speak, so that we can really identify you - Okay?" replied the manager.

Much impressed by the helpful Bank Manager, I was beginning to feel a touch intrepid as I thought about the journey that lay before me. However, I had not felt fearless and brave at a clinic where I received an armful of injections to prevent tetanus, yellow fever, cholera and typhoid.

With a very red, sore arm and a big bottle of malaria tablets rattling in my handbag, I decided to get some fresh air in my lungs.

Walking through Hyde Park, I bumped into an old Jew called Mr. Abrahams, who used to own a small London jeweller's shop near where my family lived. I was slightly apprehensive as to what his attitude would be towards me, for he must have heard, through the grape-vine, that I had been ostracised by my Jewish family following my baptism in water. However, I was really surprised to find him to be most friendly.

"How do you cope when something very unusual happens to you?" I asked, sitting down on a park bench with him.

"Oi become tremendously Briteesh. Oi always speak Engleesh. It vorks loik a dream. Ven people know you speak Engleesh den day respect yoi," he said slowly, in a broad Yiddish accent. "Oi'm not stupid, for Oi 'ave 'eard all about India, yoi know."

He stopped talking only for a moment so that he could throw some bread crumbs to the birds.

"So, yoi are going abroad, eh? Vell, each to 'is own. Dat's vot Oi always say. Each to 'is own. Oi know yoi, though. Always 'ave been a determined, independent girl. Vell, Oi think Oi'll put 2-1 on dat you vill succeed. Oi do not dink, m'dear, dat yoi vould go in for someding and not succeed."

A bet on a future missionary? It was time to bring the conversation to a close and remember that God called me to serve Him as a missionary - not as a racehorse running at 2-1 on!

The day came for the six Australians to depart from York. On their way to Folkestone they made a stop at Croydon, where they picked up their 'sheila' - *me*!

The men were still very cautious concerning their young, female companion. The coach arrived at the ferry terminal and we disembarked, each member of the party making sure that their luggage was unloaded safely.

Farewell

I had a wonderful send-off by many of my Christian friends from Bethel Evangelical Church where I had been in membership since my conversion to Christianity in 1962. They were all singing some of my favourite hymns and choruses. The minister gripped my hands and everyone closed their eyes and prayed fervently for me. Then they all hugged and kissed me. I choked back the tears as I wondered if I would ever see them on this earth again - so many dear Christians. Finally, they sang:

> God be with you till we meet again;
> May He through the days direct you;
> May He in life's storms protect you;
> God be with you till we meet again.
>
> God be with you till we meet again;
> And when doubts and fears oppress you,
> May His holy peace possess you;
> God be with you till we meet again.
>
> God be with you till we meet again;
> In distress His grace sustain you;
> In success from pride restrain you;
> God be with you till we meet again.
>
> God be with you till we meet again;
> May He go through life beside you;
> And through death in safety guide you,
> God be with you till we meet again.

They sang it over and over again until the Channel ferry departed and their singing faded away into the distance and could be heard by me no longer. I found the whole experience to be almost unbearably emotional and kept swallowing hard to rid myself of the lump in my throat.

The Australians all totally agreed at this point that they really had made a big mistake! What would it be like for them having that 'holy Joe' in tow for a minimum of three months?

The gulls screeched overhead. I took a last lingering look at Folkestone in the autumn sun. Would it be like this when I got back? Supposing I never returned? I sensed a tightening of the stomach as they cast off the last rope that joined us to the dockside.

What I had taken on was irrevocable. There could be no turning back. I had to go on. The time for talking was past, my face was set steadfastly towards India.

The ferry was almost empty - that was how much air travel was changing things. But there was a sense of ease and relaxation about being at sea.

After the Channel crossing, we boarded a train which was to take us as far as Austria with its crisp mountain scenery. During the long train journey I felt as if I should be studying the Indian language or checking timetables, but it was too late for any of that. I went to my 'bedroom' on the train and was soon fast asleep as it duly sped on.

The steward woke me gently the next morning with a continental breakfast and told me that it was a beautiful day outside.

"Where are we?" I asked, rubbing my eyes.

"The Alps, and the sun is shining," he replied.

Most important of all, we were heading east all the time. I felt as if I had finally flushed England out of my system. There was no need to look back now.

We had clocked up the countries on the train with

encouraging regularity - Switzerland, Liechtenstein and Austria.

We decided to spend a few days in Austria before boarding another train. In Vienna we had a wonderful meal - what it was exactly I cannot remember, but we treated ourselves to the works - a grand Euro blow-out! Farewell to the familiar! Not only the food and the culture, but the scenery and life itself would be very different. The leisurely crossing of Europe was a gentle introduction to all that was ahead. We were about to enter a world where things no longer happened the way they did at home in England.

The train arrived in Istanbul and we disembarked. Here we found our way to a garage in the centre of the city where we collected two extra large and apparently purpose-built Land Rovers. Before paying the owner of the garage, Steve, our vehicle expert, insisted that we were allowed a test drive. Everything seemed satisfactory and the long journey eastwards began. At the beginning, we all took it in turns to drive and, in this way, made good progress. When Steve and Roger drove the rest of us wondered if the vehicles had been modified so that the brakes and the accelerator were directly attached to the horn - very noisy!

Eventually, the driving became too tough for me, so I took on other chores, such as the washing and cooking. The driving was left to the stronger and more experienced men who were used to the rough terrain of the Australian outback.

Weariness was already settling in, which worried me for I had months of travel ahead. I did not want the men to see I was flagging and that it was all becoming too much for me, after all. Pride, I suppose!

Iraq

Iraq was then a very interesting place. I was fascinated by the people and the way in which they lived. Faces showed energy, curiosity, pride and abundant good humour. One was tempted to shed some English inhibitions and become a part of Baghdad. It was then a wonderful place to watch life; technology co-existed with the old customs. A man with a fez on his head might walk by dressed in Levi jeans and trainers - a spectrum of East and West. It was all so different from the Europe we had just left.

The call to prayer coming from the minaret of a nearby mosque rang across the city reminding us that these people were governed by 'the will of Allah'.

Parking our two vehicles, we began to look for a hotel for the night. The first man we stopped was an Iraqi who spoke English after a fashion. We resisted his invitation to show us the sights and finally persuaded him to direct us to a hotel. Getting to the hotel was not easy and I nearly walked into the traffic head on. The streets were like the Grand Prix circuit!

"You're not in London now, sport. The traffic doesn't drive on the left here, you know!" teased one of the men.

We turned a corner and found ourselves a rambling hotel that looked as if it had acne. Nevertheless, the lure of a comfortable bed and a bath was great. I had not been able to have a proper bath since leaving London.

"Have you enough bedrooms for us all?" asked Mike.

"We have eight million bedrooms," replied the hotelier.

After our laughter died down I was installed into a single room on the second floor. At the end of a long, hot, tiring day I was just longing to soak in a hot bath. I turned on the taps. At first there was a loud banging noise in the pipes and then discoloured water came out in short bursts. Some bath! Anyway, I had a bed.

This hotel, had it been in London, would have been closed down by the powers that be. But here, in Baghdad, it was of an acceptable standard!

We decided the next morning that hotels were not going to be the norm. It took too long to find suitable places. Camping out under the stars, or in the back of the Land Rover was cheaper, cleaner and safer for me; after all, women in Muslim countries usually do not go around unveiled and on their own. I was breaking all the rules! We would need to take provisions with us from now on. But what? It would be hot and there would be no means of refrigeration.

"Ah, well, start simple," I thought.

"I need to buy some rice. We are going on a long journey, so I need rice for seven people." I said to the market trader, who thankfully spoke a little English.

"I have ten kilogramme sacks of best rice," he said.

"I hope you like rice!" I smiled, turning to the six men who were waiting behind me to carry the sacks, the crates of mineral water, toilet rolls, tins of meat and everything else Western travellers seem to need. Life was introducing me to many new experiences and, working as a team to ensure our survival, was also 'good missionary training' for me.

We needed to make ourselves comfortable. As a protection from the heat a tarpaulin was placed over our sacks of provisions which made up the new floors of the Land Rovers. Great for sleeping on!

This nomadic life would, I felt, take some getting used to. I needed to remember, for instance, that the sun went down very quickly and, once it was gone, there were no electric lights!

So, immediately after tea, we got our bedding sorted out. We had to pump up seven camping mattresses with foot pumps. It was not too bad as long as we did not get a puncture! I bought my mattress and bedding in Istanbul about two hours before we left the city. They did not seem to have many camping shops and I had great difficulty getting kitted out before it was time to pack up and go. The men laughed at my beautifully embroidered pillow case, and I put up with quite a lot of good-natured banter.

"Oh, yes, very nice. Goes with my pretty blue eyes, don't you think?" joked Joe, smoothing down his eyebrows!

I bought extra blankets, but it was so hot at night that we did not need them. In a temperature of 90^0 we slept under the stars without additional covering.

One day, when travelling, one of the Land Rovers came to a stop. Steam was billowing out of the engine - all to do with the water cooling system. After what seemed an eternity, the men sorted out the problem whilst I brewed tea for everyone. Knowing I was going to India, the men often called me their 'char wallah'!

A new pattern of life began. Up at first light and a visit to the loo. The lavatory was very basic; we favoured the 'hole in the ground behind a bush' system. Using it was nowhere near as alarming as getting to it; scorchingly hot by day and suicidal at night. Nevertheless, one enjoyed direct contact with nature, but it gave 'Miss Prim and Proper', as the men called me, rather a shock for I felt very embarrassed with men in the vicinity. However, we were to be together for months and I could not wait that long!

Breakfast was always over by 7.30 a.m. and I had to

think about washing the rice for lunch before we moved off. I concocted three meals for seven of us every day. The food was simple but nourishing and no-one complained; at least not to me!

I was pleased with my culinary successes, especially when I recalled some of my disasters which happened in the kitchen in London!

We did not have many incidents of food poisoning and the kind of stomach upsets associated with the East. We were as hygienic as it was possible to be under the circumstances, but I do remember one beautiful, clear, starlit night when I was taken ill with 'Delhi belly' and needed to make several trips to the 'pulpit'; the name given to the lavatory by the Australians! At least I had the stars to guide me to the appointed place, but the next morning I was very tired.

For a while after this, just the thought of making the men their meals made me want to go home. I felt that if I stayed still and no-one mentioned food then I would be alright, but the men were unsympathetic and kept asking if I was looking forward to a nice Bombay curry!

I longed for a cool, comfortable room with a bath and a decent bed - a place to be still and alone; but this was not to be and I needed to make a recovery without them.

Every day our main meal was over by 5.30 p.m. and there was nothing else to do but to prepare for bed again. The only evening entertainment was provided by me as I washed and undressed under a long, loose robe that covered me completely from the neck down - it was held in place by a drawstring round my neck.

The men, who displayed little modesty, laughed at the wriggling that went on under the 'thing' - they laughed so much that their sides ached and tears ran down their sunburnt faces. By eight o'clock I was usually asleep on the sacks in the Land Rover whilst the men camped outside. I felt safe, unrushed and relaxed.

We made progress slowly. The heat and bad road conditions slowed us down to only 100 miles every twenty-four hours and we had to get used to not hurrying.

Iran

Crossing over the frontier into Iran, we remembered that this land, which was once called Persia, had a long history going back to the Persian Empire of over 2000 years ago. It was a land of stark contrasts. Crude oil production is the main base of the economy and the country earns great revenue from it. Yet we saw extreme poverty here which we did not see anywhere else. Most of the population is rural and very poor.

My encounter with the poor made me wish that I possessed a quick remedy for abolishing poverty. We gave some nourishing rusk-type biscuits to an Iranian family who were desperately hungry and obviously suffering from gross malnutrition.

"I wish we had so much more to give them, Joe," I said, with a feeling of inadequacy.

"If *Iran* the world..." he sang at the top of his voice with a play on the words.

"Do you always have to pretend to be so tough and void of any human emotion?" I asked him, crossly, giving his chest a push.

He just gave me a big grin. However, later, I realised just how much I had mis-judged the fellow when I discovered him hugging some very hungry children to whom he was giving candy bars and rusks.

During our travels in Iran we decided to savour the experiences of everyday life there.

"Welcome to our country," said the camel monger.

We were told by him that we would enjoy the camel ride and he promised to take a photograph of us all having fun!

"Lean back as the camel stands up and hold on tight," the camel monger instructed.

"Oo-oh! Ah-h! I don't like it! Get me off!" I yelled, when my stomach seemed to come up to my throat as the lumbering creature rose to its feet, casting a superior glance at the mortal for whom he toiled. No-one took any notice of my cries and so, looking like seven Lawrences of Arabia, we set off gingerly on the growling beasts. I suddenly knew why they were called ships of the desert - they made me feel sea-sick!

We were aware that the most difficult and dangerous part of our journey was ahead and that it would be an advantage to travel as light as possible. We were carrying too much luggage and a lot of it was mine! Women are apparently notorious overpackers and I was no exception. So, whilst in Iran, I sent all of my large luggage, mostly books, on to India. That left space enough for the seven of us, our bare necessities and basic provisions.

Our plan was that some should sleep in the Land Rovers whilst others took it in turns to drive, thereby keeping us going both day and night when passing through the danger zone of Afghanistan.

Afghanistan

Having crossed the border into Afghanistan, we were warned about the bandits that operated in the mountainous areas there. We were both emotionally tense and physically cold during this stretch of the journey. We came from the intense heat of Iraq and Iran, straight into the Afghan winter. I cannot remember another time when I have been so cold - it was freezing!

We all slept in fur hats, thick anoraks, woollen gloves, warm trousers and leather boots. We huddled together for extra warmth. It was so cold that we did not dare take off any clothing, not even to wash!

We felt relatively safe in Kabul and other large cities and towns, but elsewhere it was a very different story, and extreme caution had to be observed at all times. The tribesmen in the rugged mountainous areas were nearly always armed and we knew that bandits sometimes attacked travellers passing through. We possessed no weapons to protect ourselves so we just kept going - the men still taking it in turns to drive or navigate.

I must admit to being very scared in Afghanistan. Being so frightened made me feel a bit guilty. Was I not able to trust the Lord who said, 'Fear not'? I kept reading the words from Joshua 1:9: 'Have I not commanded you? Be strong and of good courage; be not frightened, neither be dismayed; for the Lord your God is with you, wherever you go'. I was the only Christian in the group and I was the fearful one. However, the six men did not see me as a poor witness - just as a woman who was not expected to be very tough.

Nepal

Having passed safely through Afghanistan and then the Khyber Pass, we eventually arrived in Nepal - a Hindu kingdom situated in the magnificent Himalayas.

It was here we realised our supplies of European food were running out and we were all feeling very hungry. Throughout the journey we were very careful what kinds of food we ate. Everything was boiled carefully for a minimum of three minutes. Clean water was preserved like gold dust. We never ate a salad because we did not know how it was grown or indeed, how it was prepared. No-one wanted to eat salad washed in contaminated water!

Here in Nepal everything looked very unhygienic and dirty. Nevertheless, we agreed to chance the food because we all desperately needed something to eat.

"Make sure you cook 'em well. Okay?" Ben swore at the waiter as he shouted for seven big buffalo steaks. He then looked at me, sighed and apologised for using bad language. I used to get fed up with the six men always apologising to me for their language.

"Reform would be more acceptable," I muttered under my breath.

We ate well and were apparently none the worse for eating the buffalo steaks. As we tucked into the food we talked over our adventures. Europe seemed an age away and we could hardly believe all that had happened. Whilst we talked I noticed that Tony seemed unusually quiet and almost sleepy.

"Tony, are you okay?" I asked, giving his shoulder a gentle shake. Tony was becoming drowsier by the minute. "What has he eaten that we haven't?" I quizzed the other men.

Four of them shrugged and shook their heads. However, Roger remembered seeing Tony sampling some of the local honey. That surely must be harmless enough. Tony was more than drowsy - he was slipping into unconsciousness.

One of the students from Bible College, who was two years ahead of me there, married a medical missionary and they were working together in Kathmandu. I planned to look them up during my brief stay in the country.

"Do you know where your friend's husband hangs out?" asked one of the men.

"I have an address, but I do not know how to find it. Kathmandu is a big place," I replied, as I flipped over the pages of my small address book.

"Hurry up, with that address, will you? Tony isn't getting better, you know," Joe snapped at me.

We enquired of some locals as to the whereabouts of Dr. and Mrs. Michaels and finally discovered that their home was on the outskirts of the city. After a few wrong turns we finally arrived at the Michaels' home.

"Becky! Oh, how wonderful to see you here. Bless you! When did you arrive? Oh, come in, come in!" exclaimed Pamela Michaels, giving me a hug.

"My friend Tony is sick, Pam, and we need help. Is your husband in?" I asked with great urgency in my voice.

"Yes, bring your friend in," she replied. She called to her husband to come.

The men carried Tony into the house and placed him on a couch in Jeremy Michaels' tiny consulting room.

"Mmm... yes... it's the honey. That's what's causing his unconscious state, right enough. I've seen it quite a few times before," declared Jeremy.

The contents of Tony's stomach had already been absorbed and so a 'wash-out' was useless. A drip was put in his arm and his airway was kept clear. After twenty-four hours of care Tony showed good signs of recovery and we all fussed around our beloved companion and friend as if he had just returned from the dead!

Apparently, honey in Nepal can be lethal. The bees collect the pollen from the poisonous rhododendrons which grow in profusion there, and the honey, which they make, causes severe sickness, as Tony found to his cost.

After a few days Tony improved and it was time to say our goodbyes to Jeremy and Pamela Michaels.

Whilst the men went ahead to explore the night life of Kathmandu, I stayed back for just a few hours with Pam and Jeremy who laid hands on me and prayed over me. I felt spiritually refreshed after fellowship with like-minded believers. It was good to be with them.

My Australian companions and I were together for just over three months. No one in particular seemed to be the leader, for each person in the team had a part to play. I remember Joe more than the others because of the way he challenged, teased and tormented me over my Christian commitment.

I remember vividly the occasion when Joe found a scorpion in the desert. He saw I was terrified so he surrounded it with a ring of petrol and set fire to it. Realising that there was no way out, the scorpion brought up its tail and stung itself to death.

"Hey, Becky, that scorpion is a bit like the poor heathen being surrounded by missionaries - no way out!" he teased.

I flashed my dark brown eyes at him.

It was time for me to part from the men. I was very sad

to leave the group. I trusted my life to the six men and they responded with unquestioning generosity and openness. I knew I should never again enjoy such simple and straight-forward friendships as I had made with the six men. The names of Joe, Ben, Tony, Roger, Mike and Steve will always remain in my memory. I sometimes wonder what has happened to them and whether they are now married with children. At the moment of separation it was almost impossible to think that I should never see them again. They were nice people. They hugged me and said their goodbyes.

I suddenly felt so very alone as I boarded the aeroplane to India and waved goodbye to my friends for the last time. I felt as if I were going to the Siberian salt mines as a punishment instead of the place God had chosen for me. I felt panicky and wanted to run anywhere as long as it was far away from my future sphere of service.

I was really scared. I was surprised at myself, but I now know from talking to other missionaries that this is a common experience.

The aeroplane taxied down the runway and I realised that this stage of my journey was over.

7

GATEWAY TO INDIA
(1971)

A kaleidoscope of colour and vivid images awaits the traveller to India, a complex country with the ability to steal the heart of any tourist. As a missionary I doubted whether I would ever have the time to see many of the sights of India. The time that I now possessed was my only chance.

I decided to send a wire to Claire Decker at the mission station and ask her to postpone meeting me at Bombay Station for a further week or so. I planned to see the famous 'golden triangle' of Delhi, Agra and Jaipur: a week crammed with sights and sounds which still remain in my memory, an introduction to a land far too complex to even begin to understand, but that pulled on my heart-strings at every move.

Dawn over Agra! The first red arc of sun broke over the horizon, the muezzin called and the city stirred rapidly from sleep. Raucous parakeets, green and long-tailed, swooped excitedly from tree to tree, revealing flashes of iridescent blue wings in their frantic flight.

The intense sun resembled a burning ball floating mysteriously in the midst of the air above a dusty town thrown suddenly into life. Below in the narrow streets tiny shops had dark interiors, bright lights flashed on brass scales, small boys sat cross-legged among rice and lentils, pigs foraged, cows meandered, and traders sought the shade of trees. From a jumble of houses and tumbling bricks, small girls in pristine white dresses and smart red cardigans emerged to pile into rickshaws for the school run.

Agra to me meant the Taj Mahal, the greatest monument to love. Built by Shah Jahan in memory of his beloved wife Mumtaz Mahal, who died in childbirth in 1629, it is the perfect Mogul garden tomb. Nothing could have prepared me for its beauty. None of my photographs could ever do it justice, capture the iridescence of the marble, show the exquisite detail of the carvings or the intensity of the inlays. It is, perhaps, the most wondrous sight in the world.

Next, as a sightseer, I travelled to Old Delhi with its crowded narrow streets and its remarkable Red Fort, and New Delhi, the administrative capital with its tree-lined avenues and elegant buildings designed by Sir Edwin Lutyens and Sir Herbert Baker.

Driving anywhere in India is a revelation; the roads are a tangle of hot metal, a cacophonous jungle of lorries, buses and cabs, trishaws, scooters and bicycles, and cows that wander at will through it all, somehow surviving all the noxious fumes that emanate from a forest of exhausts. "Hoot please!" exhorted signs on the back of every lorry and truck - a request happily adhered to by all drivers! On the rural roads briskly trotting horses pulled carts, over-burdened donkeys plodded along and ponderous oxen pulled their loads amid elderly tractors, while battered buses billowed black smoke, and bone-rattling bicycles rode by in single file and at a stately pace.

Travelling to Jaipur revealed another mode of transport

- camels. Not my favourite! Goats nibbled delicately at low growing bushes, cows wallowed in a muddy lake and pointy-nosed pigs scampered across roads in a flurry of trotters.

Gangling eucalyptus, tall pampas grass and flat-topped acacias grew in the dry, sandy soil where the oxen dragged home-made ploughs; roadside villages sprang suddenly into abundant colour as women in saris of luminous hues went about their daily tasks.

Jaipur was fascinating and chaotic, a people-packed trading city of constant clamour and vibrant colour. There were broad avenues and narrow passageways, a honeycomb of tiny shops, whose wares expressed the cultural diversities of India, where gold glistened, lingering spices and heady perfumes scented the air and young boys could be seen on dusty roadsides deftly stripping engines.

It was time to travel to Bombay. A delayed flight resulted in a night view of Bombay - tall buildings, bright lights and still undimmed street life.

Looking up at the clock-tower I realised that I had arrived at my rendezvous many hours too early and that there was plenty of time to see some of the sights of Bombay before meeting the mission's representative. There was no shortage of self-appointed guides to show me the tourist attraction 'Gateway to India' - a magnificent edifice, but only a gateway to those coming in from the beach.

"Would you like your photograph taken, mem sahib?" asked the 'con' man as he put his little monkey on my shoulder and pocketed the half rupee that he said it would cost. I never saw him again, or the photograph!

All the sights and sounds were a novelty to me, not to mention the smell of people and the cooking of curries at the little stalls by the roadside. Anything from a shave to a shoe-shine to a massage would be performed out of doors and witnessed by the curious bystanders who hung around.

The ever present crowd of children begging made it a problem to find solitude and so it was not without difficulty that I eventually found an unoccupied seat where I was able to write the postcards and letters that would let the praying friends back home know that I had arrived in India.

The ride on a bicycle taxi was a hair-raising experience as the driver gave me the impression that he owned the road. Motor traffic was ignored as he swerved and manoeuvred in-between cars, bullock carts and pedestrians. He had, however, a respect for traffic lights and it was comforting to know that he recognised the red light as a sign to stop! Whenever he did stop the little brown faces appeared at the sides of the taxi and the outstretched arms of children seemed to be everywhere.

"Money, mem Sahib, money," was a cry that was hard to resist. I once gave a beggar child a whole rupee without realising the folly of such an action. Suddenly, I was surrounded by many professional beggar children who were very difficult to shake off.

The need to change my European dresses for Indian saris dawned upon me following a very embarrassing incident when one little child peeped up my skirt to see if I was white all over! She disappeared as quickly as she came - her eyes the size of prunes and her teeth as white as snow against her dark skin when she grinned at me!

Bombay has a good selection of splendid hotels and I saw them during my tour, yet it was not until I walked down a side street which led behind those big hotels that I experienced a cultural shock. Down these streets the poor people were living in disgustingly filthy shacks. There was evidence of poverty and dirt all around. The stench of sewerage mingled with the smell of curry. Dirty-faced children were sitting outside on the ground eating bowls of rice. Some worn-out mothers were trying to bathe their naked, pot-bellied children by standing them in aluminium bowls and washing them down. Others were trying to feed their screaming babies, some of whom were dying from malnutrition and diarrhoea.

So much wealth was around the corner where the smart hotels were standing, but extreme poverty existed in the back streets. In some streets emaciated bodies were left to die. Flies were all over them and they were too weak to swish them away. Many were either very old or very young. As for the children, the parents found it hard to feed them, for they had already many mouths to feed, and so some little ones were invariably abandoned.

The sights of young children left to die at the end of a platform in the old Bombay Railway Station, with a piece of sacking as their only earthly possessions, was distressing. What a contrast between the breathtaking sight of the Taj Mahal and the first horrific glimpse of the underworld of poverty and suffering that is probably the real India.

I went to Bombay Railway Station to meet my senior missionary and to collect my luggage. There was my large blue trunk awaiting me which I had sent on ahead. It was mostly full of books which made it extremely heavy and I could not move it even an inch. I asked the porters if they would carry it for me.

"Oh, no, missy, this is hernia trunk!" came the reply.

Suddenly, I was aware of a white-skinned lady dressed in a pretty sari standing beside me. Her long blonde hair was plaited and fastened into a coronet style around her head. She put her hand on my shoulder. Having heard the comments about the 'hernia trunk' there was laughter in her deep blue eyes.

"G'day, you must be Becky," she said. "Come with me, please. I'm Claire Decker. How do you do? I'm supposed to be one of your 'senior' missionaries. I'm originally from Australia. Oh, and, between you and me, I don't think I'm all that senior! Welcome to India, my dear, and may God richly use you here." She gave me a big welcoming hug.

I liked her immediately and the 'G'day' was familiar to me, having spent three months with six Australian men!

We spent a short time together, allowing me to do even more sight-seeing in Bombay. The great bougainvillaea arches and the exotic eastern colours stay in my memory to this day. The time with her passed quickly by as I shared my experiences about the overland trip and I learned from her a little of what life was like as a missionary in India.

Refreshed by a cup of tea at a nearby cafe, we made our way to the Mission's old Land Rover which was parked outside the Railway Station. The eastern sun made the inside of the vehicle unbearably hot and we longed for a cool breeze. It was a long, hot, dusty trip up to the Mission Station in the Western Ghats where I would undergo an orientation course lasting twelve weeks.

The nearer I was to the mission the more I felt as if I was really going to Siberia. I shared my apprehension with Claire.

"It is too hot for Siberia!" she laughed as the Land Rover bumped along, manoeuvring round a bullock cart and avoiding yet another white sacred cow who seemed to think that India was hers.

"You know, you are bound to feel like this, for you are only human. The trouble is that Christian workers, and missionaries in particular, are regrettably placed on a pedestal just as if human thoughts, feelings and doubts never played any part in their lives," she continued.

"Well, here we are, Becky," said Claire many hours later, as she stopped the Land Rover to open the big red, rusty iron gates that led into the mission's compound.

The orientation course had such an effect upon me that I can only vaguely remember one thing - that is that couples must not walk hand in hand in the streets of India!

8

A MISSIONARY AT LAST!
(1971 - 1972)

During the long, hot, dusty drive from Bombay to the Western Ghats, Claire Decker told me many things about life on a mission station and I built up a mental picture of what I should see once the orientation course was completed.

It was not a bit as I imagined it! The shabby mission buildings, which included the hospital, were much bigger than I supposed. Claire introduced me to the other missionaries - a team of five women who were responsible for the running of the mission. They were fluent in the language and extremely experienced in the work. However, they looked very weary from almost constantly working in the intense Indian heat. Nevertheless, they put by a time to welcome me which included a special Indian meal. A little later I was to see them again in different parts of the mission, busy in the work to which I felt God had called me.

Claire took me to my quarters and gave me a couple of days to settle in before showing me around.

I do not know to this day how my 'hernia trunk' arrived there! Claire must have had more influence over the porters in Bombay than I, and someone else must have carried it from a bullock cart to my room - surely not the slight, but willing, houseboy who hovered around! I opened the sturdy blue trunk and there were my precious books, safe and sound. I never feel at home until I have unpacked my books and arranged them on shelves in a way that meets with my approval.

Anna and John, who had occupied the room previously, had kindly left behind their shelving when they packed to go on a furlough, so there was no delay in settling in.

My western clothing was packed away in the now empty trunk and I began to wear my new saris. There is a certain technique to be learned of wrapping, folding and tucking in a sari before throwing the long end over one's shoulder. At the beginning I did not always do it with the expertise that I acquired later on and there was an embarrassing moment, witnessed by the houseboy, when my sari fell off! The little Indian girl in Bombay who peeped up my western skirt had only grinned - the houseboy did not spare my blushes - he laughed loudly, shouting, "Oh, golly gosh! Look at Miss Becky! Oh, golly gosh!"

Amidst my belongings there was packed a crocheted cloth, lovingly made by one of my Christian friends as a present for me. I placed it over the blue trunk which was positioned under the window in my room. It looked very attractive.

"Yes," I thought, "this may be India, but it is also now my home. I want my room to look nice."

The presence of Claire outside my door reminded me that it was time to look around and see the work that was going on in the mission.

"In our village," Claire explained, "the natural water contains excessive fluoride and that, along with vitamin deficiency, causes bad discoloration of the teeth, especially in the five to six year olds. In an area like our's, where malnutrition is a big problem, it is difficult to isolate any one particular cause and there is very little we can do to help them. Oh, Becky, how desperately we need a dentist out here. We must make it a matter of prayer that God will send us one - one who will live by faith."

We walked across to the paediatric ward of the little mission hospital. There we saw children with swollen bellies, evidence of vitamin deficiency, eye complaints and pulmonary disease. Those little ones in care were the fortunate ones. There were a multitude of similar cases in the world outside which would receive no treatment. Claire, a trained paediatric nurse, was longing for the day when, not only a Christian dentist would come, but a Christian doctor would join the team to supervise both the medical and surgical side of the mission's work.

"We need an on-going supply of drugs and urgently," said Claire, shaking her head. "We look to be running out of most things, don't we?"

We called in at the common room for a cup of tea. After our tour in such intense heat I wanted a drink so much and I was beginning to wonder if I would ever get one! It was with a sigh of relief that I sank into an old, but comfortable, chair and reached for a cup of stewed tea, offered to me by the still chuckling house-boy.

Zilda, our senior nurse, said she would show me around the rest of the mission station. However, when the time came she was too busy, so Claire continued the tour.

"We haven't a laboratory technician," Claire told me. "And I don't know what he or she would make of this if we had one. Our laboratory is so badly equipped."

"In what way?" I asked.

"Well, see for yourself! Look at the stuff that we have

and there is no technical back-up here. We were given this blood gas analyser using radio isotopes. It's obviously useless!" She sounded disappointed.

I liked Claire very much. I felt comfortable with her. There was such a frankness about her. Most missionaries seem to be 'thankful' for everything, including the useless - not Claire! She said exactly what she thought!

Jenny, another nurse, who had been in India for only about a year, joined us. The three of us strolled across to the 'Special Nutritional Centre and Rest Home' for the elderly, the young mothers and the malnourished children.

"It's here that we supervise their recuperation," said Jenny, obviously feeling the heat - she mopped perspiration from her brow and the back of her neck with the end of her sari.

Before we entered the 'Centre' we were overtaken by some youngsters on callipers and crutches. They were a happy group and seemed to be managing wonderfully well in spite of their limitations.

"The immunisation programme came too late for some," said Claire.

"Our area was involved in a polio epidemic and there was no protection, but those kids who have suffered seem to cope very well," Jenny smiled towards them lovingly.

At the end of the tour and a hot, sticky day I was glad to retire to my room. That room, which was to be my home, was also home to bugs, beetles, fleas, lice, flies and mosquitoes and I put up a real fight to keep them at bay. When I lit my smelly little paraffin lamp and tried to read the moths became a real nuisance. They would see the light of the lamp and come circling and fluttering around it. I arranged to have a central light with a bowl of water rigged up under it. The moths, seeing the reflection of the light in the water, drowned. Well, some of them did. The others were smashed to dust by me at an alarming rate!

Before retiring to bed on my first night, the houseboy brought me a mosquito net and a very sharp knife, similar to the kind seen in an English butcher's shop. The knife was always kept within reach in case a snake or a rat invaded the room. During my years in India I thankfully never needed to use my knife, although other members in our team did. Zilda, our senior missionary, awoke early one morning to find a snake curled up beside her. With great presence of mind, she slowly reached for her knife and, with one swift movement, cut the snake into pieces. The worst moment in the whole episode was when it was served up in a soup for the evening meal!

Much to learn! (1972)

"DOCTOR! DOCTOR!" someone shouted, banging loudly on my door.

I have never been very good at getting up once having retired to bed, but this time there was no choice - the banging was not going to stop!

I slipped on my long, pink, cotton dressing gown and brown leather sandals. I rubbed my eyes, trying hard to shake off the feeling of sleepiness.

"Who are you? What do you want?" I shouted back through my door.

"Hurry, please, doctor," pleaded a man's voice.

"I am *not* a doctor," I said slowly, "I am a missionary - a nurse and a midwife."

"You must come, doctor," shouted the man, who was still banging on my door.

As I gingerly opened the badly fitting door, a strong, dark, hairy hand quickly gripped my arm.

"Girl much sick!" shouted his companion.

I grabbed my medical bag and flashlight and went off with the two strangers. They half dragged me out through the compound's gates and pushed me along the dark narrow streets. I was taken to a wooden shack with a corrugated iron roof upon which the moonlight shone.

Inside was a girl of about thirteen or fourteen years of age. "What is the matter with her?" I asked in my new language, shining my flashlight into the darkness of the squalid, cramped room.

Quickly, they told me her story. At the age of twelve years this girl was sold to the priests in the Temple for prostitution and, after a year with them, she became pregnant. The baby, now ready to be born, was coming feet first instead of head first - a delivery that is not always easy in an ideal western setting, let alone in a remote Indian village. The most senior woman in the village declared herself an 'expert midwife'. When the baby's foot appeared, this self appointed 'expert' said that it was 'of a devil' and promptly cut off the baby's little limb, leaving one dead infant still not born.

The young mother was grossly dehydrated and very close to death. Moving her could put her into further shock and cause her to die. I had to take a chance for I could do nothing for her in such dark, unhygienic conditions. I requested that the men carry the young girl to our inadequately stocked 'delivery suite' at the mission station. There was so much blood everywhere - her's and the baby's and I needed to be able to examine her properly in a very good light. They shook their heads because those

Asian men rarely went near women in labour.

"DO IT NOW!" I commanded at the top of my voice, stamping my foot. It was done, but not without a lot of verbal abuse from them. We hurried back along the dark narrow streets and through the compound's rusty gates with a much greater sense of urgency than the men who sought my assistance a little time before.

The 'delivery suite' was very different from the clinically clean and well equipped one in the east London hospital where I trained as a midwife. The floor in our mission's 'delivery suite' was a dirt one with a covering of manure mixed with tea leaves! The mixture was effective as a dust controller but, oh, the smell!

The frail little body of the girl was placed on the delivery table. Two other missionaries turned out of their beds to assist me - Joy, a teacher, and the other Claire, a trained paediatric nurse. The young houseboy also helped by swishing any flying bugs away from the patient.

A little gauze mask was placed over the girl's face by one of my 'assistants' and the smell of chloroform began to pervade the place, nullifying a little the smell of the manure. On examination I discovered that the dead baby's shoulders were stuck.

"Oh, what a mess! I will have to crush the shoulders in order to get this baby out..." I began.

"Becky, forget it. She's gone," Claire interrupted, a sadness in her voice.

The young mother's life had slipped away.

From the day of her birth until the moment she passed beyond human help she was part of a way of life with nothing to commend it. I failed to save her. I was saddened even further by the realisation that the opportunity never came to tell her of Jesus, the sinner's friend. And now it was too late.

I went outside the building to tell the news to the villagers who were noisily crowding around outside the compound. News seemed to travel fast in our village! Although we had made many friends amongst the people who lived in our remote village, there were also those who were eager to stir up trouble for the mission. We were disliked by all of the Hindu holy men and the minority of Muslims in the community were very hostile towards us. The situation could have turned nasty at that stage.

"This foreigner is not a doctor," shouted one man, angrily, "She's a fake!"

I was thankful that I learned their language back in England and was able, with a fair amount of fluency, to explain to them what happened. It was a real relief that there was no violent disturbance.

"May God have mercy on your souls," I said, raising my right hand.

The crowd began to disperse at the call of another woman who removed any remaining tension by turning to the crowd and saying, "Never mind. Come away. What is all this fuss about? The dead girl was a 'nothing' anyway. Who cares?"

Sickness, death, helplessness to save the body, difficulties in communicating the gospel to hostile people in order to save their souls, so that one watched body and soul pass into darkness from which there is no return. The need! Oh, the need!

Next morning, Zilda came to see me in my room about the events of the night before. She sat on my bed and, in a way that did not arouse any ill feeling whatever, gently reprimanded me about the way I reacted to the urgent summons from outside my bedroom.

"I realise that you are new to life out here, Becky," she said. "I appreciate your motives and what you did to try and save that young mother's life, but never leave the mission compound at night on your own. If you have to go out then get someone else up to go with you. Okay?"

She went on to explain that it might not have been a genuine call for help at all, and to go outside the compound at night in the company of two unknown men was sheer folly. She told me that it was not unknown for people to go missing in India and she did not want anything like that to happen to me.

I realised there was much for me to learn about many things. However, one thing was quite certain - I was a missionary at last!

Men only

The company of those six Australian men on the journey to Asia was in stark contrast to the company of my five missionary colleagues who were all women. Sometimes, on the journey to the East, situations arose which called for the kind of physical strength which is usually the possession of many men, but few women. Driving over difficult terrain, changing wheels on the Land Rover or moving boulders from the roadway were things that the Australians took in their stride. Men's work! I played my part by doing some driving, cooking meals or acting as the group's medical adviser, but it was a comfort to know that there were men around.

The five women at the mission station were a strong team. Attractive, slim and feminine, they nevertheless taught themselves to do what some would call 'men's work'. Wheels on the Land Rover were changed with zeal and dexterity, heavy boulders were somehow moved aside on the unmade roads of rural India and, when the road ran out and the Land Rover could go no further, they would hoist up their saris to knee level and tramp across the rough fields to visit farmers who may have contracted leprosy.

I became the sixth member of this female team, sharing in the work and ministry of the Christian church but, although there were men on other mission stations, we had no male member to help us and there was work to be done which is considered by some church leaders to be the task of *men only*. In the absence of male workers, there is only one alternative to leaving the work undone and that is to go ahead and do it!

Whenever Christians gather together to celebrate the Breaking of Bread, the Lord's Supper, the Holy Communion, or whatever other name they choose to call it, the sex of the celebrant is a thorny issue. Whenever our Field Superintendent decided to pay us a visit we assumed, quite naturally, that he would lead the worship, preach the Word of God and officiate at the Lord's Table. It was good to have this man around, but his visits were only occasional - about twice a year. Most days we gathered together in the evening to hear the words, "Do this in remembrance of Me," and to break bread together in the presence of our risen Lord. On these occasions Zilda would take over the leadership of our gatherings and bring the elements to us.

On a Sunday morning, Indian Christians were made welcome at the service and, providing they were true believers, they were invited to share in the Breaking of Bread. On these occasions we took it in turns to officiate and did not feel that we were trespassing in a sphere of ministry that should be labelled *men only*.

We practised only one mode of baptism and that was by immersion in the river. In Hindu society this is seen as a decisive step and is only performed when someone makes a profession of conversion, showing evidence that they are Christian disciples by openly destroying their Hindu idols. Only then are they considered candidates for baptism. The destroying of Hindu idols can arouse fierce hostility from the immediate family of a convert and one of the men baptised by me in the river was later put to death by his brothers. There were no witnesses. However, it was thought he was knocked on the head, ferried out into the river in a small rowing boat and thrown overboard.

During my stay at the mission station I witnessed about 30 baptisms in the river and all were, with the exception of one, performed by the women. One baptism coincided with the visit of the Field Superintendent and he, naturally, took over.

Baptising by immersion calls for a certain amount of physical strength and could be considered *men's work*. In some baptisms in the Western world when the candidate is a hefty man or buxom woman I have seen men double up to make sure they had the united strength to lift the new convert back out of the water. In poor Indian villages overweight persons are hardly ever seen, so candidates for baptism were usually thin, wiry people. Some of the stronger women taking a baptismal service could cope on their own. It is a thrilling sound to hear the words ring out over the river bank: 'On confession of your faith in the Lord Jesus Christ, I baptise you in the name of the Father, the Son and Holy Spirit'.

There was no indigenous church exactly where we were. There certainly was in many other parts of India for years and years before and with national and international structures. However, our mission was an inter-denominational Faith Mission and so we formed our own little Bible-based chapel for the new Christians. Its human leadership? The women, of course!

In 1947 India was given her independence and the British presence was slowly disappearing. We wondered what the future held for missionary societies in general and ours in particular. Would the time come when missionaries would be withdrawn from India just as they had been from the great country of China? Some members of our mission experienced difficulty in getting their visas renewed and this led us to think that our days there could be numbered. We already realised how important it was to train workers from the ranks of the local Christians. One of our team was very gifted in training Bible-women and she trained herself to sit cross-legged on the ground for long periods of time so that she could instruct them without too much discomfort!

It was a great day when a well educated Christian believer moved into our locality. He was a high caste Hindu who moved away from another town because of the hostility from his family and, together with his wife, took up residence in a house near the mission station. He was fluent in English and offered his services to the mission. It soon became apparent that this man showed the makings of a good Christian Indian pastor, but how could we train him? What did the apostle Paul mean when he wrote to Timothy: 'I permit no woman to teach or have authority over men; she is to keep silent'? Whatever the interpretation, we realised that we must do something.

We arranged a correspondence course with a Bible Institute in the United Kingdom which was very helpful. Even so, he needed the help of our lady missionaries in working his way through the course. He gained practical experience in communicating the gospel when he came with us to our open-air evangelical outreach meetings during the Hindu festivals and also amongst the crowds in the local bazaar.

We played gospel records on an old wind-up gramophone and joined in the singing ourselves. This 'noise' always attracted curious on-lookers. The Hindus enjoy music but did not always interpret the words as one intended them to be understood. An example of this was when I was singing along with a gospel hymn which said, 'Bring me water, water, the water of life', without realising that the words could be interpreted literally until later on when the record was being played to a queue of out-patients at the clinic. Then some well-intentioned Hindu women took their pitchers to the river and brought me water!

Our Indian helper was able to get the message across without being misunderstood in this way; his command of the language being a very real advantage. Opportunities to preach in the Sunday services were given to him and our fellowship of lady missionaries rejoiced to know they played some part in the steady development of this man into a fully accredited pastor.

Dressed in 'best clothes', missionaries from the different mission stations met together in a nearby town for the Indian man's ordination service. The Field Superintendent presided over the gathering and, in an atmosphere of worship and thanksgiving, we felt so glad that, whatever the future held for our mission, a real move had been made towards a strong indigenous Christian church.

That dreaded disease (1973)

During my second year as a missionary, I was sent to Vellore Hospital, which is in the south of India, to engage in a three months intensive course on leprosy. This enabled me to gain enough experience to be appointed for the post of senior leprosy worker near Bombay. I then often had the delightful privilege of issuing to former leprosy patients an all-important certificate stating that they were free from the disease. Although one did not use the word 'clean' as in New Testament times, to be declared free from it was a happy experience for them. In practice, however, the Certificate of Health was not always acknowledged. So great is the stigma surrounding leprosy that fearful people follow the maxim, 'once a leper always a leper', and they were sometimes forbidden to ride on public transport or meet in public places because of the obvious disfigurement left by the disease.

The crack of dawn heralded the start of a working day for me. I marvel now that I used to get out of bed at 4.45 a.m. to meet the farmers in the fields around 6 a.m.! After a cup of tea and a cookie, an Indian worker and I would climb up into the Land Rover and bump over the unmade roads to a point as near to the farmer's field as possible. We would call out to him and, more often than not, he would come over to meet us. This leprosy work was performed in conjunction with the Indian Health Authority and it was to them that I had to send the medical records and reports. Only occasionally did I have to pull rank and tell a farmer that, if he did not comply with government policy, I would have to bring out a government official to see him. On the whole there was a willingness by the farmers to be examined for signs of the dreaded skin disease. I would look for early signs of the disease of lepromatous leprosy - always a slight thickening of the skin on parts of the face and ears with loss of the outer portions of the eyebrows; there were also faint pigmentary changes in the skin, visible in good light.

When the signs of the disease were in evidence it was necessary to go to the man's home for an examination of his wife and family. They invariably manifested character-istic skin changes to confirm that the loss of facial hair was in fact due to leprosy. Babies were not born with the disease, but living in contact with those who had it, in poor, dirty conditions, meant that, sooner or later, they were likely to contract the disease themselves.

The tablets I gave to my leprosy patients were effective, but the side effects of the drug made some people very ill. In the mission hospital I was in charge of a ward of about 20 beds reserved for leprosy patients who could not cope with the side effects. If the patient was a mother breast-feeding a baby, then I would help out at feeding times and bottle-feed the little one on milk that was kept in the breast-milk bank.

I would not allow them, however, to bring in their Hindu idols. As a Christian mission we enforced a policy of no compromise with idols and encouraged those who wanted to follow the Lord Jesus Christ to turn away from such man-made things and destroy them.

Whenever we had a vacation we usually spent it at another mission station. When it came to my turn to have a few weeks off I chose to spend it in Madras where our oldest active field worker was living. She was a friend to us all and a 'mother in Israel' to many new recruits. She was Auntie C. to everyone in our missionary society.

People say you know nothing about India if you have never been on a train. My journey to Madras, therefore, had to be by one! Some such journeys can take many days. I remember this one very well.

The sun was high as the train clattered through the red fields on its way to the south. The compartment had filled up during the night of the journey. A fat grandmother had spread herself on the seat opposite. A man with a long, black moustache snored in the luggage rack above. Then from down the corridor a new noise started up. Two children appeared - a little boy with a huge accordion hanging from his neck, and his sister. The girl shut her eyes, tossed back her head and sang, 'You are my sunshine, my only sunshine', while doing a sort of dance in the narrow corridor. When the song finished she went around the compartment holding out her hand for money.

"Shoo! shoo! Go away!" said the fat grandmother.

The little girl stuck out her tongue and the two scampered off down the corridor with wicked grins on their faces!

The train began to slow down. A small station was approaching - just a local stop. Still there was plenty going on - people coming and going.

I jumped down on to the platform, taking a water bottle with me. A man with a cart piled high with soft drinks pushed his way through the crowd calling out the prices in a singsong voice as he went. I was just putting on the cap of the water bottle at the drinking fountain when the Station-Master clanged his bell, the guard flapped his flag, the train jerked into action and started moving off slowly. I broke into a run and hopped on to the footplate at the very last minute.

After that excitement a man came round selling tea from a huge tea-pot. He was followed by a young girl selling sprays of jasmine for the hair. The fat grandmother wanted the jasmine. I asked for tea. Soon the tiny compartment was as busy and as bustling as the station itself.

Finally, it settled down again to the clickerty-clack music of the train wheels. A white shrine in a field flashed past. A line of white birds slept on the telegraph wires between the poles. A group of children and a man with a bicycle waved from the barrier of a level crossing. They were there and then they were gone.

The train carried me to the station I had been waiting for - where I had to change trains. There were people selling things and passengers chasing porters who ran ahead with luggage perilously perched on their heads.

However, above all the noise and the hubbub there came from the end of the platform a hiss of steam and a long, high whistle that shook the birds out of the sky. The air became hotter and the steam cleared. There stood before me the most magnificent steam engine I had ever seen.

The engine driver leaned out of his cab.

"Hey! I have to change here. Are you going to Madras?" I called.

"You had better climb aboard because steam trains don't wait for anyone - not even you, mem Sahib!" he yelled back, giving me a big wink.

It was wonderful for me to finally reach Madras and be in the company of dear Auntie C. There was so much to say, for we had not seen each other for well over a year and she wanted to catch up on all my news and what was going on in the area where I worked. It was lovely to have fellowship and prayer with that dear old saint.

Next morning, when we sat together at breakfast, I asked if I could wander around Madras.

"I am a little too weary to take you sightseeing. Are you able to go without me, dear? I'll send one of our reliable Indian Christian workers with you so that you will not be completely alone. Okay?" she said.

I agreed and my Indian companion and I set off together to see where East meets West. It may now be the film capital, the Hollywood of South India, but colourful Madras, an amalgamation of modern industry and ancient culture, established in 1639 as the British East India Company's first trading station on the east coast, still had many recognisably British buildings.

They were laced by wide roads of fast moving traffic and tiny, narrow backstreets teeming with vibrant life. Men wore white dhotis or lungis and women moved gracefully in saris of brilliant contrasting colours in a climate that went from hot to hotter. Palm and casuarina trees edged the mile-long marina, an esplanade where university colleges, and a circular Victorian ice factory, faced out over a wide beach and the calmly lapping Bay of Bengal.

Although evidently a stronghold of Hindu culture and tradition, I was amazed to discover that Madras had quite a large Christian population, witnessed by the many churches in daily use. How unlike the remote village where I was stationed!

"You must be tired after all that sightseeing. Come and have some tea with me," said the elderly missionary.

I sat down at the table. Sitting opposite this white-haired lady and chatting to her, it slowly dawned upon me that something was not quite right. The outer parts of her eyebrows were missing.

At no time during my leprosy work was I afraid of the disease. It had never occurred to me that any member of the mission would contract it, but I was now mistaken.

Breaking it to her as gently as I could, she gave me permission to give her a check-up. Sure enough, there was the evidence. She was a leper. Fortunately, the dreaded disease was not so advanced that there was loss of sensation in her hands or feet. However, it was the end of an outstanding missionary career. She never wanted to leave the India she loved, but there was no other alternative. The Field Superintendent was informed.

Auntie C. was started on a course of D.D.S. tablets whilst arrangements were made for her return to the United Kingdom. She received treatment at the Hospital for Tropical Diseases in London and then went to a home for retired missionaries. She never saw India again.

9

SLIPPERY SLOPES
(1974 - 1975)

I worked very hard for three and a half years, engaged in evangelism, midwifery and leprosy work, mostly on the hot, dusty plains of India. Towards the end of the three and a half years I, too, was taken ill - nothing whatsoever to do with leprosy, though!

The mission's superintendent felt that I should rest up in the hills where the vegetation was lush and the air fresher. He arranged for a Christian doctor to see me there, who diagnosed severe amoebic dysentery, bacillary dysentery and hepatitis 'A'. Complications arose which were affecting my body's vital organs, the lungs in particular.

"She could be treated in Bombay probably quite successfully," the doctor informed the superintendent.

"Probably? Oh, no! This mission has a policy not to take risks with a missionary's health. She is only six months away from her first furlough, so I think that it would be wise to send her home prematurely. She can have the best of care in London and combine it with an early furlough," the superintendent said adamantly.

My physical condition was rapidly worsening so I was taken immediately from Heathrow Airport as an emergency case to the Hospital for Tropical Diseases in St. Pancras, London, and I was there for quite some time undergoing tests and treatment. Following my admission, when I was very poorly, the medical treatment made me feel weaker than ever and it was a while before there were any obvious signs of improvement.

My main objective was to get well quickly so that I could return to India - the land I had come to love and regard as my home. No longer were the people there foreign to me with strange customs, language and food. They were 'family' and I desperately wanted to rejoin them and continue my ministry there.

However, I was not coping with the way the illness, and the sheer fatigue that accompanied it, was affecting me spiritually. I suppose, like many other Christians, I did not fully understand the interplay of body, mind and spirit which made for good health. It seemed at the time to be just a spiritual low and I tried to deal with it as such.

I called for God but my prayers seemed to ascend no higher than the ceiling of the hospital ward. I wanted to know He was around and to experience His presence. Perhaps the psalmist felt like this when he wrote: 'Why are you cast down, O my soul, and why are you disquieted within me?"

There was apparently no immediate answer to my cry for help and prayer seemed to me like a waste of time. I was being nursed in an isolation ward and was conscious of the comings and goings of doctors and nurses in green gowns and masks, but the sense of His Divine Presence, so precious to a Christian, was denied me.

I am by nature a private person and do not find it easy to confide in other people. However, I plucked up sufficient courage to send a message to a minister of my acquaintance with a request that he come to visit me. Surely, I reasoned, the wisdom and prayers of an older experienced Christian will be of help. My message arrived at the manse at a time when he was up to his eyes in work and he was too busy to come.

I knew that my whereabouts were known to the staff at the mission's home base in London and I was hoping for a visit from someone there but, for some strange reason, no-one came. Maybe they thought that they would be infected!

I did not expect anyone during the afternoon's visiting time and so decided to have 'forty-winks'.

"Becky, wake up! You've a visitor," said the Ward Sister, giving me a gentle shake.

I rubbed my eyes. There, standing by my bed in the hospital's white mask and green gown, was my friend Helen! We shared a room together during our three years general nursing training. I had not seen her since a year after Sophie's tragic death in 1967.

"What are you doing here?" I asked happily, propping myself up a little in the hospital bed.

Plumping up my pillows before sitting down on a chair beside my bed, she told me she had read in the mission's newsletter that I was ill and so enquired further as to my whereabouts.

Helen peered at me over her white, hospital mask.

"You do look a mess. My word, you look an awful mess. Look at your hair! And your skin and eyes are the most terrible yellow colour," she continued bluntly, "You've turned from a grape to a raisin!"

I explained all that happened to me.

"Well, my girl, I am going to take you in hand when you are discharged," she said firmly, spraying my wrists with her expensive perfume!

"Mmm ... that is a lovely perfume. What's it called?" I asked, smelling my wrists.

"You're changing the subject," she reprimanded. "I mean it ... you're going to stay with us ... and it's no good shaking your head."

"Look Helen, I do appreciate it, but, as soon as I am well again, I'll be able to sort myself out and return to India. Don't worry about me, darling," I said. "I'm a tough old boot!"

Being Helen, she took absolutely no notice and, when I was finally discharged from the hospital, insisted that I spent a time convalescing with her and her family.

On my return from India the sum total of my belongings consisted of two pretty saris, a few nighties, some underwear and a pair of worn out sandals. The rest of my belongings were in my room at the mission in India.

Helen and her husband took me to Marks and Spencers in Croydon. There I was kitted out with the latest western fashions in clothing. It was strange to be in European dress once more - all those collars, buttons, zippers, belts and tights!

One day never to be forgotten, whilst staying with Helen, the postman brought me a letter from the Indian Embassy. I tore it open eagerly knowing that it was something to do with a visa application for my return to India. My heart sank within me when I read the words: "Your visa application has been refused." Disappointment and sadness filled my mind and heart.

Going to my room, I caught sight of myself in the mirror and began to reminisce concerning my time in India. It seemed like yesterday that, as the mission's newest recruit, I was overwhelmed with the enormity of the task before me and felt like 'doing a bunk'. So much was packed into those three and a half years - failures and successes, tragedies and blessings.

My thoughts were interrupted by Helen's voice.

"Becky! Come down and join us," she called up the stairs. "Someone wants to meet you."

I did not really want to go down and meet anyone, but I could not be discourteous. I tidied myself up and went down to the lounge.

"This is our pastor's mother. She is visiting her son and his wife for a couple of weeks," Helen's husband informed me.

I shook hands with the smart, elderly lady and we sat down in the comfortable green armchairs. Helen went to the kitchen in order to make some coffee.

"Where do you come from?" I asked the minister's mother.

"Oh, I originate from Nottingham, but my husband and I have retired to a little bungalow in Worthing. I hear that you are a missionary in India," said the visitor, changing the subject. "Are you here just for your furlough? Do tell me!"

"I don't want to tell anyone anything yet," I thought to myself.

"No. It seems that I am not any more!" I replied, hoping that the conversation about my past would not develop. I felt sick at heart and did not want to talk about what came in the post.

"Oh?" she enquired, leaning forward in her chair, obviously eager for me to tell her more.

"I was in India for three and a half years but came home because of illnesses I picked up out there. I've heard this morning that they won't renew my visa to return. I don't know why because the need for missionaries is just as great now as it was three and a half years ago," I said, trying in vain to satisfy the guest's curiosity about me.

"You were only three and a half years out there you say?" she asked.

"Yes," I answered monosyllabically, hoping the topic of conversation would change.

"My dear, were you sure that you were really meant to be in India then?" she questioned, "After all, it wasn't very long and now no visa ... well?"

Her remarks were not meant to hurt, but they did. I knew that my call to go to that land was definite and clear. What was happening in my experience now was anything but clear. I politely excused myself after a second cup of coffee and sought my own company.

It was a joy for Helen and I to meet Janet at Victoria Station, London. She was a fellow missionary who was home on furlough from another of our mission stations. We were all friends and went for a simple meal at the 'Golden Egg' cafe just along the road. She told us the latest news concerning the mission and how the proposed amalgamation with another small Faith Mission came into being during the time I was in hospital. I was experienced in working with Hindu people whereas she worked amongst the Moslem community. Now that her furlough was nearly over the mission was sending her back - not to India, but to a new work in Iran, and her visa was granted.

"Look, do you mind if I leave the two of you for a while? I want to do some shopping in the Army and Navy Store and Selfridges. Okay?" Helen asked, explaining further that she would return in about an hour's time, which really meant two hours at least!

Janet and I ordered another pot of tea. I was able to confide in her about my situation and the effect that it was having on me.

"I am feeling very fed up. I really want to be back in India. A short furlough's okay, but I want to be overseas. I don't belong here in the U.K. any more. India is my home now. What am I to do?"

"You can't storm the Indian Embassy and make them give you a visa, you know," Janet reasoned. "If you can't get a visa, then, well, you need to come to terms with it, Becky. Forget it!"

I did not intend to forget it. I reapplied several times for a visa. The mission also tried to assist me concerning the acquisition of a visa. It was hopeless and, eventually, I realised that the door to India was closed to me. I cannot confess to having been less than heartbroken. What of the work out there? Who would take over the leprosy work? The mission's representatives in London reminded me that the work was the Lord's - not mine! They asked me to become involved in deputation work for them, taking meetings throughout the U.K., thereby stimulating interest in the mission and its work. I could have worked for them, saying all the right things, but I knew that my spiritual life was a mess. I could use 'the language of Canaan', but my heart was not right before the Lord God.

Resigning from the mission, I determined to get away from it all and go to some place where I was unknown. My faith was shaken and I was so weary that I was prepared to give up the spiritual struggle. It seemed as if God had let me down. These were slippery slopes indeed!

The next few weeks were spent job-hunting and I

eventually found a post as a junior lecturer in Nursing Studies.

"Rather unexpected, isn't it?" asked Helen, "Are you really sure that you honestly want to leave us and go north?"

"Yes, Helen, I'm sure," I replied. "I've spent long enough under your roof. I can't express how grateful I am for your hospitality and everything else you have done for me, but it's time now for pastures new."

I was putting on an outward holy act in front of other Christians, but, inwardly, I was like Jonah of old - on the run!

Restoration and renewal (1975)
It was the middle of January and the snow lay deep on the ground. I shivered and pulled up the fur-trimmed hood of my coat.

"Eee, lass, thou dost look snug under that hat," said the old man to me in his strong Yorkshire accent as we boarded the over-crowded lower deck of an old red and cream-coloured corporation bus. I had arrived in the north of England!

I started my new post as a lecturer in Nursing Studies. The salary was quite good and I was well able to afford the rent on a very spacious and luxurious apartment in a smart suburb of the industrial city. Materially, I was fairly well off. Spiritually, I was fast becoming a pauper.

Quite deliberately, to avoid anyone in my social circles assuming that I was a Christian I purchased a packet of twenty cigarettes and left them on the coffee table in the lounge of my flat. The cigarettes remained unopened. I just felt that, on seeing them, visitors would not engage me in conversations about spiritual matters or my past.

The unopened packet of cigarettes was hurriedly thrown away one day when a missionary friend from India, who was nearing the end of her furlough, telephoned to say that she was in the area and wanted to visit me. It was good to see her but I had to put on an act, using the language of Canaan, when talking to her. How dishonest!

For about eighteen months my life was spent with worldly friends, both male and female, at noisy parties, unhelpful films or beautiful concerts. Then my two closest friends both informed me that they had gained promotion in their chosen professions and it meant that they would have to move away.

Suddenly, due to their absence, my social life took a rapid nose-dive and I began often to feel so extremely lonely. I remember coming home from work one day, making myself a meal for one, and sitting down alone in front of the television set. There was nothing on to interest me so I switched it off. The room took on an uneasy silence, and I felt so isolated in my apartment. I felt unwanted and unknown and longed for companionship.

Two older lady acquaintances did call in once or twice a week and their visits were welcomed, but the sad and widespread malady of loneliness is not dispelled with a little chat now and again. It was hard at the end of the day not having someone with whom I could talk. The newspaper, the book, the little walk, the visit to the shop - how unsatisfying they were! How futile!

God allowed me to follow my self-appointed lifestyle long enough to realise that being offended with Him and His people had absolutely no future at all.

One Sunday at 8.30 p.m. I turned on the radio and was surprised to hear the most beautiful hymn-singing. The room was filled with the haunting words of William Cowper's lovely hymn: 'Where is the blessedness I knew when first I sought the Lord?'

I sat down and stared out of the window. I realised how lonely I was without the fellowship of my Christian friends. I also realised that I needed the blessedness of the Lord, His joy in my life. Leaving the Lord brought only unhappiness. I knew that I needed God as I had never needed Him before, but He seemed so far away.

"That's it," I thought. "I'm going to rectify this situation."

I picked up the Yellow Pages and looked under 'Churches'. There was the telephone number listed of a Baptist Church. I decided to dial without delay.

"Hello, this is the caretaker. Can I help you?" asked the slow voice of a Yorkshireman.

"Will you give me the telephone number of your minister, please? I need to contact him," I said.

Having the minister's number in my possession it took me at least three weeks before I eventually plucked up courage to telephone him.

"I hope you don't mind my telephoning you. I know how busy, as a minister, you must be, but I really do need help," I said, nervously.

"Oh, that's okay. We ministers only work on a Sunday, you know!" he joked. "What can I do for you?"

Two hours later, I found myself sitting in his study. It was a dim, shabby room in need of decorating and the furniture had seen better days. His books seemed to be everywhere in untidy piles. His big old desk was equally very untidy. I wondered how he found anything when he worked in such chaos. However, he was a warm, gentle man and his face shone with the love of Christ. I felt immediately at ease with him.

"How can I help you?" he asked kindly, sitting back in his big comfortable-looking, old armchair.

I blurted out my story, feeling more than a little guilty. I told him how sad I was because I would not see India again. I confessed that God was no longer allowed to be part of my life. I told him everything.

He was thoughtful for a few minutes, then frowned and stared downwards.

"Well," he said, "the problem is that many Christians put ministers, and missionaries in particular, on a pedestal. They forget to toil in prayer for Christian workers who are in the front line of battle - and it is a battle, too! They rarely think that those of us in full-time work ever experience immense spiritual difficulties, do they? Anyway, we mustn't blame our 'prayer partners' too much, must we? What you experienced was close to a bereavement. You think that you've lost all by being away from the India you love, don't you? What you need now is to just simply rest in God's presence. You might not be able to 'feel' the Lord, but He is there just the same. He loves you. He really does."

"I was taught that I should read my Bible and 'pray without ceasing', but I can't," I interjected, near to tears.

"Yep, that was good advice, but for the time being, let me do the praying! It won't be long before prayer and the Word of God will become real to you again. What you need to focus in on is the fact that He loves you - that's the main thing. You may have tried to shut Him out of your life, but He loves you so much that He knows even how many hairs you have on your head and that's a good few more than I have!"

He was right, for, as we prayed, the Lord's presence seemed to fill the room like a sweet-smelling perfume. No longer did God seem out of reach. I experienced joy unspeakable and full of glory!

10

TELLTALE EYES

I was wondering what sort of spectacles would suit me best, when the adjoining door opened and I was called in to see the optician.

After chatting a while about nothing in particular, he began his examination by peering into my eyes with his opthalmascope.

Then the conversation took an unexpected turn.

"How long have you been a diabetic?" he asked.

"I'm not a diabetic," I said with a grin.

"You surely must be because you have a degree of diabetic retinopathy," was his firm reply.

I was not surprised at what the examination revealed, but for some strange reason I did not tell him that my telltale eyes were now a testimony to Divine healing rather than Diabetes Mellitis.

My mind flashed back to April, 1979 when, at the age of thirty-two years, I began to lose weight. I also consumed gallons of tea, coffee or water in an attempt to quench the thirst that kept returning.

I arranged an evening appointment to see my medical practitioner in his surgery.

"You can go in now," said the receptionist, pointing the way. "It's the first door on the left."

I felt a little nervous as I entered his consulting room.

"Sit down, m'dear, and tell me what's wrong," he said,

glancing at my medical records.

"I've lost two stone in weight over the last two months. I am so tired and I cannot quench my thirst," I stated.

He did a quick medical test which showed a vastly abnormal amount of sugar and ketones in my blood.

"Well now, it's obvious what's wrong with you, isn't it?" he said, for he knew I was medically trained.

"You're going to tell me that I am a diabetic, aren't you?" I asked.

"I am so very sorry, Rebecca, really I am," continued the doctor. "I will arrange for you to see a senior physician at the general hospital."

I came out of the surgery and sat in the passenger seat of a friend's car. The friend, who was waiting outside the surgery, quizzed me as to what was wrong.

"Please, just take me home. I need to be alone," I said, feeling as if I had just been given a life sentence. "I need to get my thoughts in order."

The following Tuesday came and I went to see the Senior Physician at the local general hospital. The blood tests confirmed that I really did have Diabetes Mellitis. He prescribed 12 units of Actrapid Insulin and 24 units of Monotard Insulin to be given by daily injections and he insisted on my having a 160 gram carbohydrate controlled diet.

"There's no reason why you cannot live a perfectly normal life, you know," the physician said, obviously trying to reassure me.

"I hope so, but I cannot see my life in the future ever being the same again, can you?"

A 'perfectly normal life' was something I certainly did not have. I became a 'brittle' diabetic, which meant that there was the likelihood of reacting to the insulin, or going into an insulin coma very quickly.

On several occasions I woke up in a hospital ward and once I nearly died. I carried chocolate and glucose tablets in my handbag, but could not always do anything to help myself because of the confusion that accompanied the onset of an insulin reaction.

One day, while crossing a busy main road on my way home, it occurred to me that, if I did not have something to eat quickly, I might be in trouble.

Reaching the island in the middle of the road, I stood and fumbled in my pocket for a sweet, but there was nothing there. I was beginning to feel distinctly queasy. I opened my handbag for some chocolate but it had been eaten the previous day and the supply was not replaced. I looked in another compartment of my bag for a glucose tablet, but found the last remaining one in an inedible powdered form. I was becoming confused. I needed something to eat - and quickly. I tried to cross the road but I was too confused to reach the other side. I stepped out. Cars hooted and some drivers yelled at me. I staggered back to the island.

Two policemen saw me as I dropped to my knees on the island, my hands in the dirty wet road. They tried to pick me up and, thinking I was drunk, bundled me in the back of their car and took me back to the Police Station.

What a smell! I looked around. Where was I? There was a bed standing in half of the small room. Upon the bed was an old, worn, grey and navy blue blanket and a striped, stained pillow without a pillow case. In the corner was a metal bucket! There were bars at the window and the strong sunlight shone through. The door was wide open and a tall, middle-aged man stood in the entrance.

"What on earth? Am I in a prison cell?" I asked, my voice gradually becoming louder, "What have I done?"

"Are you feeling better then?" enquired the man.

"Who are you? And why am I here?" I yelled.

"I am the police surgeon. Fortunately for you, the desk sergeant was an observant man and he noticed that, instead of sobering up, you were getting worse. It so happens that his daughter is a diabetic and something must have clicked in his mind. Quickly, he searched through your handbag and, finding your diabetic card, he called me. I gave you an injection to bring up your blood sugar. You must now have a big drink of milk and then we'll arrange for you to have a high carbohydrate meal. Okay?"

"Okay," I replied, "but I want to get out of this horrid, stinking cell. It is really bad. Ugh!"

The surgeon laughed and called for a young constable, who was very kind and rustled me up a three course meal in the police canteen. I began to feel so much better.

Although the police apologised for putting me 'inside', the incident was not without its humorous side. Together we laughed about the tea-totaller who was wrongly committed to a cell for drunkenness!

Occasionally I attended a Pentecostal assembly when the weather conditions prevented me from driving across the town to the Baptist church. At the Pentecostal church I grew accustomed to the way that sick people were invited to come forward for healing. The pastor and elders would lay hands on the sick and sometimes wonderfully miraculous things happened. But not always. It was not an uncommon sight to see disappointed people taking their infirmities and sicknesses back home again.

What I did not like there was the way the unhealed were blamed for not having enough faith to be healed. It was pathetic to see some sick people trying desperately to obtain more faith, or analysing their faith, in a hopeless effort to discover its deficiency and thinking this was keeping them from the healing power of God.

There is, I feel, a real mystery about Divine healing. Paul said that he left Trophimus at Miletus sick and he prayed to the Lord three times for his own healing, but received his answer in the words, 'My grace is sufficient for you.' To blame a sufferer for lack of faith is cruel, and it is not an answer that satisfies me.

However, God is good and does not refuse to work because the emphasis is not quite right. On about six occasions I too went forward to receive the laying on of hands without anything happening whatsoever. Then, in the November of 1979, the conviction was borne in upon me that I was only wanting healing to get rid of the inconvenience of being a diabetic. I felt that healing would only take place when I wanted it all for the glory of God.

One Sunday evening, as the service drew to a close, the invitation from the letter of James was given: 'Is any among you sick, let him call for the elders of the church and let them pray over him, anointing him with oil in the name of the Lord; and the prayer of faith will save the sick man.' I went forward yet again and the pastors and elders laid hands on my head and prayed.

My healing took place there and then, but I did not know it. There were no feelings or any indication that anything had happened. Next morning I gave myself an insulin injection as usual and quickly went into a coma. I was admitted to the general hospital as an emergency.

"Why on earth did you give yourself insulin?" I was asked. "A healthy person cannot tolerate insulin."

When I saw the physician and told him what happened, he performed a glucose tolerance test upon me which was normal. He confirmed that I was no longer a diabetic! He was at a loss to understand it with his medical mind, but could not deny the reality of the healing. He wrote to my General Practitioner that they had 'witnessed a miracle'!

Standing up to testify to God's power to heal was something of a thrill. There was only one thing that cast a shadow over the occasion and that was the face of a doctor friend. He was a diabetic and a man of faith who was not healed. How I wished that he stood with me, saying the same happy things that I was able to say, but it was, for some inexplicable reason, not to be.

11

THE WARDRESS
(1981)

I walked into the morning service and sat in my usual seat, which was situated on the right-hand side of the church. My friend Janet usually sat beside me, but she was away on holiday and so the chair was left empty. I took off my coat and gloves and piled them on to the empty seat next to me. It was the custom in that little chapel for everyone to be seated at least ten minutes before the service began and, mainly to prevent idle chatter, everyone joined in the singing of choruses:

> He lives! He lives! Christ Jesus lives today!
> He walks with me and talks with me
> along life's narrow way.
> He lives! He lives, salvation to impart!
> You ask me how I know He lives -
> He lives within my heart.

We were just singing it through for a second time when a visitor walked in and, seeing the empty chair next to me, asked if it was reserved for anyone. I shook my head and pushed my coat and gloves on to the newly carpeted floor beneath my seat.

Just over an hour or so later the service was brought to a close and the pastor was standing at the door, shaking hands with the congregation as they filed out. The women seemed anxious to leave for they were worried that their prepared roasts which were cooking away in their ovens would end up as burnt offerings!

I held back to greet the visitor who had sat next to me. She was a thin, tired looking woman probably in her late sixties. Her eyes lacked lustre and her skin hung in empty folds around her neck. She smelled of a cheap perfume.

"It is good to see you here. Have you come far?"

She explained that she rented a small apartment about two or three miles away and she lived alone. As she spoke I noticed that she had a heavy foreign accent.

"Where are you from originally? I hope you do not mind me asking."

"Oh, I am from Germany," she replied.

"Really? That's interesting. My paternal grandfather came to England with his wife and five children from Germany just before the outbreak of the Second World War. One of the five children was my father. It is quite a story!" I remarked.

"Why did they come to England? Why did they flee from Germany? Were they not loyal to our Fatherland?" she asked.

"They loved Germany, but they were Jews ..." I began.

"I *now* understand," she interrupted. "So *you* are a Jewess?"

"Yes, of course. I was born a Jewess and I will die one. I am a fulfilled Jewess for I found the Messiah in 1962. I know Him as my own personal Saviour. The Messiah is the Lord Jesus. I am now a Christian, but being a Christian doesn't mean that I am not a Jewess any more. No! When a Jew believes in the Messiah Yeshua (Jesus) he or she returns to the God of Abraham, Isaac and Jacob - fulfilled and completed. It is wonderful!"

She frowned again at me and lowered her eyes.

"Is something wrong?" I quizzed, trying to gain eye contact with her.

"Have you heard of Belsen?" she asked.

"Who hasn't? Virtually the whole world has heard of that place. Ugh! Do you know my father nearly died there? He was captured during the Desert Campaign, put into a prisoner of war camp and, when he was found to be Jewish, he was taken to Auchwitz and then on to Belsen. He was German but acquired British papers and so that was why he was with the British Army. Anyway, why do you ask if I have heard of Belsen?"

"Well, you see ... oh, how can I tell you this? I was a wardress in the women's section of Belsen. I used to tell the women - Jews, of course - to strip themselves of all clothing and go into the showers. They were not showers, but gas chambers. If they had children then they were to hold the children very close and were to breath deeply. It was I who led thousands of Jews to their death. I was one of the most cruel of all the wardresses. Now, here we are in a church together - ex-wardress of Belsen and a Messianic Jewess! Both Christians, eh? God has forgiven me completely for what I did ..."

"Stop it! I am sorry, but I don't want to speak with you. I am going home," I snapped.

The pastor was still at the door but I unwittingly ignored his outstretched hand and went off to sit alone in my little blue mini for about a quarter of an hour. Finally, I started up the engine and drove towards my home. On the way I saw the German lady standing at a bus stop. She flagged me down. I stopped.

"What do *you* want now?" I yelled out of the window.

"There is no bus for another two hours. I've just missed one. I do not know how to get home. Please, I am sorry to ask this of you, but would you give me a lift in your car? I have arthritis in my feet and it will be painful to walk too far."

I felt my adrenaline race and I was angry. "I am sorry, but I will not give you a lift. Do you know why? The reason is that six million Jews were killed by people like you. One million were babies and children. You personally were responsible for thousands. Look, you made my people walk to their death. No, Fraulein, you can walk ... not to your death, but to your warm, clean apartment which is free of dirty water, rats, fleas, leeches and the smell of death and decay. I am a Jewess born in 1946 - a year after you were killing Jews. Ugh! Go away, you ... oh, go!"

I drove off leaving her standing at the bus stop.

Reaching the next roundabout I decided to return to where the German woman was waiting. I would give her a lift. I would not have to speak to her but I could at least drive her home. To leave a woman stranded in the cold for two hours would be inhumane on my part. I had not considered that my behaviour had already been inhumane.

I arrived back at the bus stop, but she was gone. Surely, she had not attempted to walk all the way to her home with such severe arthritis. I knew roughly where she lived and so I began to drive slowly along in that direction. Nothing. I could not find her. Maybe another motorist, kinder than I, felt sorry for her and gave her a lift home. Maybe she hitched a lift and some weird man picked her up. She could be in immense danger.

Why am I bothering about her? She didn't bother about

what happened to all those dear, but terrified, Jewish women and children who she sent to the gas chambers. How could she have done such terrible things? She must have been completely evil. Forget her! I thought to myself.

The Lord brought to my mind the chorus which we had all been singing at the start of the morning service...

"He walks with me and talks with me..."

I was not allowing Him to talk with me regarding loving that wardress. I closed my mind and took on board the haughty attitude that she should not have dared to speak to me of all people, as if I were, for some reason, superior because I was a Messianic Jewess - one of God's elect.

"He lives within my heart."

Really? Someone was living in my heart, but the Lord was not being allowed much living space.

At 6.20 p.m. I was once again in my usual seat ready for the 6.30 p.m. start of the evening service. I peered at the empty seat at my side. I was oblivious to the chorus singing and wondered if the German woman would come again. What a mad thought! After the despicable way I treated her that morning she was unlikely to ever show her face again at our chapel.

During the evening meeting there was a communion service. As the pastor led the people in worship he gave out the cautionary word of warning as found in 1 Corinthians 2:28,29, and made it clear that this also applied to Christians who had a grievance against another brother or sister in Christ.

How could I partake of the Bread and Wine after my behaviour towards the *ex*-wardress who was now my sister in Christ? If I let the elements pass me by I would feel that everyone would notice. After all, it was such a small assembly. I would stand out like a sore thumb and some would quiz me regarding my actions. No! I would take the elements. Anyway I could not put it right with her for she was not there. I would just pray up an arrow prayer to my Heavenly Father through the Lord Jesus Christ and everything would be just fine. Wrong!

'If you do not forgive men their trespasses,' Jesus says, 'neither will your Father in heaven forgive your trespasses.' Forgiveness is a direct act of the will.

"Father, please really forgive me and help me. With all my heart, I am sorry," I prayed with tears in my eyes.

Suddenly, I experienced God's love in an intense way. In my own strength I did not have love. Neither did I have the power to love. The power to love came to me from the Holy Spirit, 'because the love of God is shed abroad in our hearts by the Holy Spirit which is given unto us' (Romans 5:5).

I went home that night and prayed that I would be able to meet the Fraulein again just so that I could ask her to forgive me. That was back in 1981 and I have never seen her since.

12

TWO ARE BETTER THAN ONE
(1982 - 1983)

In 1982 I decided to resign from my post as a lecturer in Nursing Studies and I happily returned once again to hospital work as a Sister on a medical ward. My new post was in a large teaching hospital about forty miles away. Shortly after taking up the new job I moved into a modern three-bedroomed, semi-detached house built on the edge of a high moorland village - about twelve miles from the city's hospital.

I felt that I should integrate myself into the life of the village, so I started by going along to the local Methodist church. It was very different to anything with which I was familiar. I was used to charismatic Bible-based churches - this seemed anything but! In my opinion they appeared to concentrate too much upon the social functions and jumble sales. I was inwardly critical of their whole set-up.

"It's virtually dead!" I muttered to myself after I left the morning service. "If it is no better this evening I'll drive into the town next Sunday."

The evening came and I again took my seat in the little village chapel. I was pleased that it was a different preacher. "His style of preaching is what I've grown accustomed to, and he's obviously very Biblical," I thought. "I like him." I began to think more favourably about the village church!

After the service I went to shake hands with him, but he

turned away to speak with someone else, so I did not know who he was.

During the week that followed, I met the superintendent minister who had the oversight of the village Methodist church. It was a chance meeting in the street.

"Who was the preacher on Sunday?" I asked. "The one who preached in the evening, I mean!"

"Oh, that was Mark. He's a lay preacher," explained the minister.

During the conversation with the superintendent I learned a little more about Mark. I learned that he was a bachelor living with his widowed mother. He was once a student and then a member of the evangelistic staff at Cliff Bible College. His hobby was photography.

A couple of weeks later I met up with Mark at a mid-week Bible study held in the house of a local evangelical believer.

"I hear you are a keen photographer," I enquired after the meeting when we were all drinking coffee.

"Oh, yes, very much indeed!" he said, enthusiastically. "What about you? Do you enjoy photography?"

I told him that I recently acquired a 35mm camera. With that, he asked if I would like to go to Sheffield with him and help photograph the cathedral. I accepted his invitation, explaining that I was very much a novice with my new camera.

Various outings followed, and we decided to continue our friendship. Love between us quickly blossomed and, one evening when we met, having told me again that he loved me, Mark went down on one knee, which made me laugh, and said, "Darling, will you marry me, please?"

I accepted his proposal of marriage and we celebrated

our engagement with a superb meal at a smart restaurant. The candle-light threw a warm and rosy glow over the scene which seemed to be a reflection of my inner feelings for him.

What began as a friendship was now a romance - a romance for life! We began to make plans for a summer wedding.

From the moment we announced our engagement, life became a matter of decisions, an exciting whirl of plans and preparations: my dress; my shoes; a bridesmaid; the cake; the flowers. And our first home: colours, fabrics, patterns, plates, china and glass, table linen, pretty sheets for the bedrooms, carpets for the floor. But what to choose? Where to start? I always seemed to be in a hurry. There was so much to do.

One day, I rushed to meet Mark so that we could attend a church service together. During the service I looked down at my feet and, to my horror, I realised that there was a blue shoe on one foot and an identical grey shoe on the other! From that time on Mark and I tried to slow down somewhat and keep all our plans completely God-centred.

Our wedding day eventually arrived.

The beribboned white Rolls Royce drove me to the picturesque setting of a little Methodist chapel situated on the outskirts of Dewsbury in West Yorkshire. The chauffeur followed a delightful route along country lanes, avoiding the industrial area in the valley below. The friend who sat beside me and who was to give me away cracked jokes to try to calm my nerves!

The torrential morning rain stopped and the sunshine began to break through the clouds, turning an unpromising start to the day into a glorious afternoon.

The official photographer was waiting. I do not like having my photograph taken, but there was no escaping on this day, and I very much wanted a photographic record for posterity. He was not the only one with a camera. Some of the local residents were congregating around the gates of the chapel with their little compact cameras. It seemed that everyone wanted a photograph! I felt my face aching as I kept up a smile for the popping flash-bulbs.

The minister who was to conduct the service of marriage was at the door of the chapel to greet me. He kissed me on the right side of my face and told me that I looked lovely. My unruly curly hair was 'tamed'. My long pink and white dress in satin and tulle cost really more than my then nursing salary allowed! Groomed to almost perfection, I felt unusually shy and self-conscious as I was not used to having all eyes on me in such a way.

I walked slowly down the short aisle and stood before the Communion Table. The minister, a tall man dressed in a long black cassock, belted at the waist, peered over his glasses and smiled warmly, obviously still trying to put me at ease. I was, as a speaker, used to standing before larger congregations than the one now assembled behind me, but this was different. I really was full of the collywobbles!

The man about to become my husband stood on my right. Seeing him made me relax. There were no doubts. He was God's choice. He was the man for me. His smile told me that he loved me. He loved me and I loved him.

Suddenly, I collected my thoughts as the minister said: "We are gathered here in the presence of God to witness the marriage of Rebecca and Mark, to support them with our prayers and to share their joy. Marriage is given by God. It is not to be entered upon or thought of lightly or selfishly, but responsibly and in the love of God. According to the teaching of Christ, marriage is the lifelong union in body, mind and spirit, of one man and one woman. It is His will that in marriage the love of a man and woman should be fulfilled in the wholeness of their life together in mutual companionship, helpfulness and care. By the help of God this love grows and deepens with the years. Such marriage is the foundation of true family life and, when blessed with the gift of children ..."

The unexpected (1983 - 1984)

To be perfectly honest, almost everything in my life has been unexpected and the thoughts that were buzzing around in my head following the wedding ceremony were truly unexpected. The minister who conducted the service read from the service book, 'Such marriage is the foundation of the true family and when blessed with children...'

Blessed with children?

When I was in my twenties I longed for a baby so much that sometimes I could hardly bear the frustration of being childless.

I was thirty-seven years of age. Mark was even older. To start a family at our age seemed to be foolish. I tried to consider realistically what it would be like to have a child - to live with it day by day and, worst of all, night by night!

Mark and I openly discussed most things together prior to our marriage, but the subject of a child never came into our conversation, so I needed to find the right moment to bring up the subject.

"Oh, but having a baby would be lovely. It would be

our baby - ooh, Mark, just think ..." I began one evening.

"I am thinking - about the realities, which are a bit more complicated. It would be with you twenty-four hours a day, seven days a week, when you are tired and when you are ill, and when you are distracted and when you are weak," replied Mark, shaking his head. "And what is more, we are a bit old to start a family."

"I think it would be wonderful to be pregnant and to know I'd be going to bring a human being into this world," I said, looking like a dejected bloodhound.

Mark remained unconvinced.

I went to see our General Practitioner about another minor matter and asked him if I would be wise to have a baby. "I'm thirty-seven. Is it crazy to think about getting pregnant at my age? Could I have a less than perfect baby due to my advancing years?"

"You are a medically trained person and you know that the answer is 'yes' to both your questions. But you are obviously determined to have a baby and listening to reason won't stop you! In fact, if you get pregnant we will assure you of the very best of obstetric care. Okay?" came his reply.

All I needed to do was to convince Mark!

Four months later I felt very unwell and began to be sick. All I wanted to eat was porridge or salad cream sandwiches! I could not face a cup of coffee. I only wanted to drink pineapple juice or cold cocoa! The doctor hardly needed to confirm, to our great delight, that I was pregnant. Together Mark and I began to look forward to the time when we would welcome into our home a little baby.

The pregnancy seemed to us like a major miracle. The first time I felt the baby move inside me, something primal and immeasurably important happened in my innermost self. I, with all women, of all time, felt utterly and irrevocably female.

I remember many feelings. Some confused, some startling. I had a strange feeling of invasion - another living being was temporarily inhabiting my body and I loved it.

I was frightened of what was happening and of the unknown. Was it possible to be this nauseated and still live? I was also apprehensive about my time in labour and the pain that would accompany it. I was fearful in case my baby was abnormal. All this turmoil was going on, of course, at the same time as I was growing smugly proud of myself for being pregnant. To me it was as amazing as life on another planet.

However, the pregnancy did not progress as easily as I hoped and I needed to spend sixteen long weeks in bed. Because of my age and the problems that were arising throughout the pregnancy, I always saw a senior obstetrician.

She was an unattractive woman. In fact, the first time I saw her I thought she was a man until I noticed her skirt! She shouted at almost everyone, especially the Pakistani men who brought their wives to the ante-natal clinic. The Pakistani men would occupy the seats in the waiting room whilst their tired, pregnant wives would stand up. This would enrage the obstetrician - she would shout at these men and make them wait outside. Her language at the time was invariably very bad, but she called it 'colourful'.

Most of the midwifery staff and the junior doctors who worked at the clinic were apparently as unnerved by this female as I was. One member of the staff would keep an eye out for the arrival of the obstetrician. When her car

156

pulled into its own private parking space, all the staff would take up their positions. She would then march in, not stopping for anything or anyone that was in her way and the work would begin in earnest.

Towards the end of my pregnancy, I was breathlessly lying flat on my back on a couch in a cubicle of the antenatal clinic waiting for the obstetrician to come.

She duly arrived and began to examine my 'bump'.

"How old are you? Thirty-*eight*! You must be mad!" she said, still pushing my 'bump' around. "Why have a first baby at your age?"

She told me that the baby was coming feet first and that she was unable to make it turn around to ensure that it would be head first. In her usual direct way, she told me that I would need a Caesarean section due to the position of the baby. She obviously could not put the baby of a thirty-eight year old woman at risk by allowing her to go into labour and deliver a breech. So it made sense for me to have a Caesarean section.

I went home with the obstetrician's words still ringing in my ears: "There's not an obstetrician in the country who can turn that baby. It's a fixed breech!" Mark tried to comfort me, without success. I was not open to reason.

That evening we went to a prayer meeting at the Methodist church where we were members. The minister and his wife Anne were parents of two-year-old twins and we were able to share things with them. After the meeting we stayed behind for a coffee and I told them that I was to have a Caesarean section because the baby was a breech.

"Would you like Anne and me to pray?" the minister asked me in his quiet voice.

I was surprised by the suggestion. After the obstetrician's authoritative pronouncement, it did not occur to Mark and me that it was a matter of prayer, for it was so final.

"If you want to," I replied with a sigh. "Why not?"

They prayed and, as they did, the baby seemed more active than ever. This also seemed to increase the heartburn and breathlessness from which I suffered during the latter part of the pregnancy.

The following week I, still with my 'bump', waddled along to yet another ante-natal check up.

Once again I climbed breathlessly on to the couch and awaited the arrival of the obstetrician.

She marched into the cubicle and began to feel how the baby was lying.

"That's funny," she said. "Most odd!"

"What is?" I asked.

She ignored my question and called for the senior midwife. Complete panic seemed to fill my whole being. Whatever was wrong? Why was she calling for the midwife? Why would she not answer my question when I asked what was wrong?

The midwife came and palpated my abdomen. She agreed that it was funny.

Why would they not tell me what was 'funny'?

"What's wrong?" I asked in a louder tone. "Tell me, please!"

"Nothing, absolutely nothing!" came the reply from the obstetrician with a smile.

She told me that the baby had turned, although it was actually too big to do so. It was now coming head first instead of feet first and so I would not need a Caesarean section. I would have a normal delivery unless, of course, anything went wrong in labour.

"I don't understand how that could have happened, though," said the obstetrician, frowning and shaking her head.

I explained that the minister and his wife had prayed with me about the position of the baby. I waited for the reactions from the obstetrician and the midwife.

"Well," replied the obstetrician, "I never believed in God, but no-one else could have turned that baby. There isn't an obstetrician in the country who could have turned the baby. It was too big to actually turn around by itself. It must have been your God."

The obstetrician then turned to the midwife and asked her if she believed in God.

The midwife shuffled her feet and looked embarrassed.

"Well?" bellowed the obstetrician, "Do you?"

She suddenly remembered an urgent job that just could not wait and rushed away!

On the following Friday morning at 6 a.m., I began to have severe backache. Then the contractions started. I told Mark it was time to go to the hospital. He raced to get the car out of the garage. My small suitcase was thrown onto the back seat. Then he realised that it would be a good idea if he put me in the car, too!

The hospital was a long drive from where we lived and we seemed to catch every red traffic light along the way!

On arrival at the hospital, I was taken to my own private room where I was examined. The contractions were coming thick and fast, but they were not causing the labour to progress. At 3 p.m. I was given medication to rectify things. It worked!

The midwife was suddenly assisting the delivery of our baby whilst Mark was still trying to tie up the back of her sterile green gown. At 3.25 p.m. a baby cried. We had a son! And it was a normal delivery! It was a happy day - one to treasure for ever, even though it seemed long and arduous for me. The midwife began to tell Mark to give me a kiss. She was too late. I was holding our new son in one arm and my other arm was round my husband's neck as he kissed me. He was so overcome by the whole emotional experience that I could feel his wet salty tears on my face.

We were now a family.

Timothy was fine, weighing in at 8lb. 2oz. on 31st August, 1984.

An angel? (1984)

We used to have a little golden haired Cairn terrier whom we named Jenny for no reason at all. She had been cruelly treated by her previous owner and, when we first approached her, she cowered in the corner of the room. It took quite a while for her to completely put her trust in us. She eventually came to the conclusion that anyone who took her out in all weathers at the drop of a hat could not be all bad, unless, of course, they were completely mad!

One day, after my lunch, I decided to put my feet up and rest for a while. I was about 30 weeks pregnant and feeling the heat of the June weather. Jenny scratched at the door and then, after circling around a few times, whined at me.

"Oh, no, Jenny, I'm too weary now to go for a walk. You can just go for a run in the garden."

The front garden was long and enclosed by five foot high fencing. She would surely be safe enough there. Mark and I had planted some Rosa Regosa plants - the prickles from them were quite sharp. I let her out and a few minutes later I heard her yelping. Jenny had managed to catch herself on the prickles. I picked a couple of thorns out of her fur and stroked her coat. She seemed unhurt.

"Come on then. I'll take you for a walk."

She jumped up around my legs in excitement as I fastened the lead to her collar.

"You won't be able to demand a walk just when you feel like it when the baby's born. There's a lot to do for a new baby," I said, just as if she understood!

We walked along past all the newly built houses. In the front garden of one of the larger houses there was a smart middle-aged lady attending to the weeds. She looked up and smiled at me.

"I don't know where all the weeds come from!" she said, making polite conversation.

She stood up, held on to her back and stretched.

"You shouldn't be trailing your dog around in your condition on such a hot day," she added.

"Probably not, although she wanted to go for a walk. The exercise will more than likely do us both good. I did have other plans however, like sitting with my feet up in the cool of our lounge. I'm feeling the heat just now," I replied. "And I've my own built-in central heating!"

"Would you like to come in and have a cold drink of my home-made lemonade? We are new around here and I would value the company, dear."

I agreed, for I was also new to the area.

I sat down in Maureen's large, comfortable lounge while she washed her soiled hands in the kitchen before pouring out the most delicious, ice-cold lemonade.

"Sorry to have kept you waiting," she said, handing me a full glass. "When's your baby due?"

"Oh, not until the end of August. I'll be glad when the

pregnancy is over, too - forty weeks seems an awfully long time to wait, doesn't it?" I replied.

"Is it your first baby?"

I nodded. "Yes, we only married eleven months ago."

"I hope you won't think me rude, but aren't you taking an enormous risk at your age? After all, there is the possibility of having a baby suffering from Down's Syndrome or spina-bifida when you are older, isn't there?" said my newly found Job's comforter.

I finished the lemonade and made movements to leave. I knew all too well the risks of having a baby in later life, but all my ante-natal tests showed that our baby was normal. I explained this to my hostess, but she, of course, knew women who had abnormal offspring, despite their check ups, and proceeded to describe their physical and mental distresses.

That evening at about 6 p.m. Mark returned from work and asked me how I was.

"Okay, I suppose. Bit fed up. I dunno," I said, shrugging my shoulders.

Mark frowned and put his arm around me.

"Do you want to tell me about it?" he enquired. "Or shall I leave you alone?"

I swallowed hard to rid myself of the lump in my throat and reached across to the box of tissues to blow my nose and wipe away the tears which were welling up. I told Mark that a woman had invited me in to her home and flooded me with stories about other women's abnormal offspring.

"Supposing our baby is abnormal ... after all, I *am* now thirty-eight and there is bound to be a risk ... How would we cope? Oh, Mark!"

"Hey, hey, now stop it. You know, our baby will be fine. Okay?" he said in a firm, comforting way. "Would you like me to go and speak to her and ask her not to upset you in this way again?"

I shook my head. I composed myself again and I remembered when I was working as a student midwife learning about such foolish women who plague mums-to-be with horror stories about other pregnant women they knew who had suffered, or with old wives tales. As prospective midwives we were trained to reassure our patients and quell such nonsense. However, I was no longer the midwife - I was the patient, emotionally involved and it was awful.

Whenever I happened to see Maureen I deliberately kept the conversation light, usually talking about the weather.

Timothy was born, and was just perfect - in fact, he was absolutely beautiful! One day, soon after having come home from hospital, I was upstairs in Timothy's room. I had fed him, changed his nappy and tucked him down in his cradle for a nap. What a good, contented child!

"Becky, Maureen is here. May she come up and see Timothy?" Mark called up the stairs.

"Sure. Send her up."

Maureen came up and peered into the cradle at the sleeping Timothy who had neither spina bifida nor Down's Syndrome despite my advancing years!

"Oh! He is just adorable!" exclaimed Maureen who was completely oblivious of the stress that her thoughtless words once caused me. "You'll have to look after him well. After all, haven't you read about the number of cot deaths that have been reported lately in the press? There have been babies dying by the age of six weeks," she said, still living up to being the present-day Job's comforter.

"Maureen, don't say such things. I can't bear it," I pleaded, tearfully.

I knew that Maureen's words were stupid, but my hormones were not allowing me to behave in a reasonable manner. I used to creep in and stare at Timothy just to check that he was still breathing. When Timothy was six weeks I watched over him even more, pleading maybe a little irrationally with the Lord not to take our only son. That night, after putting Timothy to sleep I saw standing behind his cradle a tall, glorious, colourful being whose brilliance I could not measure. I was stunned and amazed and could hardly stand the sight of it. And then it was gone. I knew that I had seen an angel guarding over our son.

"Ha," laughs the sceptic. "She has recently given birth to a baby and her hormones, not yet back to normal, are playing havoc - probably suffering from post-natal depression and seeing things."

Not so! General William Booth, founder of the Salvation Army, stated clearly that he saw angels which were surrounded with an aurora of rainbow light so brilliant. Was he mad? No.

I opened my Bible and read from Daniel 6:22, 'My God hath sent His angel, and hath shut the lions' mouths.'

Truly God had sent His angel. Timothy had his own personal angel in heaven. This angel always saw the face of my Father in heaven (Matthew 18:10). Wonderful! And, as for shutting the lions' mouths, well, we never heard Maureen's tales ever again.

After Timothy (1984)

A few years after his conversion to Christianity, my husband began to take an interest in things Jewish through the influence of an inspiring preacher called Ernest Lloyd who, like me, is Jewish - a Hebrew Christian.

My husband feels, as I do, that there are many customs and practices belonging to God's ancient people that could well enrich those who belong to the Lord Jesus Christ.

It is the custom of a Jewish midwife, at the birth of a baby boy, to throw a prayer shawl around the shoulders of the little one and to recite the SHEMA (Deut. 6:4-5 A.V.).

When Timothy was born the setting was wholly Gentile. The midwives were splendid, but the only Jewish midwife around was myself and, as an exhausted new mother, I was only too glad to rest. However, Mark, remembering this practice, said to Timothy the first words he was to hear:

Hear, O Israel, the LORD our God is one LORD, and thou shalt love the LORD thy God with all thine heart and with all thy soul and with all thy might (Deut. 6:4-5 A.V.)

After my few days' stay in the maternity hospital, Mark came to take me and our new born son home.

I knew that, as parents, our responsibilities towards our child were threefold. We were there to protect him from all that was harmful, to provide for all his needs, and to prepare him for adulthood.

Although I was trained as a nurse, midwife and community nurse, looking after my own child was not as easy as giving advice to other people regarding their children!

There was a time when Timothy hardly seemed to eat anything and this was a cause of real concern at the time.

The more we fussed about it the worse he seemed to become.

Others to whom we talked treated it lightly and always said the same thing: "When he's hungry, he will eat!"

When I flip over the pages of the photograph album and I look at the pictures taken of him during this period I wonder why we were so anxious, for he looked to be a happy, healthy little boy.

Years before, when working as a community nurse, I called on a family whose baby had been injected against whooping cough. She reacted in an adverse way, leaving her with brain damage. Never again did I want to witness that kind of distress.

When the time came for Timothy to have protection against whooping cough, Mark and I were in a dilemma. We knew how serious it was to contract this infection, yet the memory of what happened to this other family haunted us almost continually. We talked about it with other parents and asked a paediatrician what he thought. After deciding not to allow it, we changed our minds and, with great trepidation, went along to the surgery to have him immunised. What a sigh of relief went up when everything turned out satisfactorily!

The daily grind of housework was interrupted one day in a surprising and delightful way. I received a telephone call from the obstetrician who cared for me throughout my pregnancy.

"I can't forget what happened. You know, when that minister and his wife prayed and your baby turned from a breech into a cephalic presentation," she said.

"Oh, yes, it was great, wasn't it?" I replied.

"Well, I've been thinking, it must have been God,

mustn't it? After all, I couldn't turn the baby."

"Yes," I said again.

"Will you please send me some information about God? I don't want you pestering me. All I'm asking for is a small amount of literature. Nothing else. Okay? Send it care of the hospital. It will reach me," she stated, and quickly put the telephone down before I could say any more!

I sent her a John's Gospel and a small booklet which was an explanation about the Christian faith and how one should respond to it.

About a month later she telephoned me again and asked where she could get *lots* of Christian literature!

"I've given my life to the Lord Jesus Christ and I want plenty of literature to give to all the staff at the hospital," she said, enthusiastically.

It transpired that she attended a Billy Graham Rally at the football stadium in Sheffield and went forward at the close of the service to make a public commitment to Christ. A couple of weeks later she gave out Christian literature to many of the hospital staff, telling them in a way that was more of a command than a suggestion: "You must read this!"

Tact was sadly missing in her attempt to witness!

When I came into contact with this great character, she was near the end of her working life and was making plans to retire to New Zealand where her Christian sister lived.

Only once was I to meet her again. She was over in England on a visit and, quite by chance, we met in a Christian bookshop. It was good to see the change in her life and to hear first-hand of her involvement in the worship and witness of a lively church in New Zealand.

After that exciting interlude we continued to live out

our days in a quiet sort of way, worshipping together on a Sunday, entertaining now and again, but giving our family life, after God, the central place.

Parenthood, we feel, is an important and God-given role, and the awesome responsibility of it all makes us aware of our need of help from the Father above. That help has been forthcoming as the following incident will show.

A very large, heavy picture used to hang on the wall above the spot where Timothy's high chair was positioned in the kitchen.

"I feel sure that picture is unsafe," Mark said one day.

"No, it's fine. I put it up myself," I answered.

"Yes, I know. That's why I think it is unsafe!" he replied with a grin. "I'll have a look at it when I've a bit of time."

Sure enough, during the night, the nail holding up the heavy picture pulled out of the wall. The huge picture crashed down and we found it next morning on the floor behind the high chair. At breakfast-time Timothy would have been lifted into his high chair for me to feed him. If he had been sitting there when the picture fell it would have caused him to sustain serious, if not fatal, injuries. Coincidence? No! It was the Lord's protection upon that young life.

In our parental role of protecting, providing and preparing I would like to stress the importance of praying. Both Mark and I have prayed, and will continue to pray, that Timothy will be used for God's glory throughout his life.

13

SEVENTY TIMES SEVEN
(1991)

The B.B.C.'s nine o'clock news finished and the television in the lounge was turned off. I felt a little chilly and wondered if seven-year-old Timothy was warm enough, for he still often kicked off his bedding when he turned over. I crept silently into his bedroom. He stirred a little in his sleep as I tripped on a small toy car which had not been put away in the toy box. I pulled his continental quilt up over him and Toby who is an old, very lovable bear.

"Is he okay?" Mark asked, as I came down the stairs. I nodded.

"You know, Becky, I have been thinking about the whole business of forgiveness." Mark leaned forward and asked, "Do you think it is more difficult for Jewish people to forgive than for Gentiles? Is it a racial problem? Is there something about the Jewish nature in that they cannot forgive?"

"Well, Peter was a Jew and he asked the Lord how many times he should forgive those who wronged him. He took it for granted that he was to forgive. He knew he mustn't bear any grudges or try to take revenge, but forget any injuries. He thought that to forgive seven times in his life would be sufficient. Jesus' direct answer to Peter was that he should forgive seventy times seven! Wow ... that's a total of ... er ... 490! In other words there is something of an ill nature in scoring up the injuries we forgive. God multiplies His pardons and so should we," I replied.

Mark frowned and was thoughtful for a few moments. He got up from his chair and walked across the lounge to the bookcase. He thumbed through a commentary by William Barclay.

"You have only been reading from Matthew's Gospel, but Barclay comments from Luke 17:4. He says, and I quote: 'Verses 3 and 4 speak of the necessity of forgiveness in the Christian life. It tells us to forgive seven times. The Rabbis had a saying that if any man forgave another three times, he was a perfect man. The Christian standard takes the Rabbinic standard and doubles it and adds one. It is not a matter of calculated arithmetic. It simply means that the Christian standard of forgiveness must immeasurably exceed the best the world can achieve'.

"So, really, all Jews know that they should forgive, but, after all their sufferings, it may be all to do with the individual's personality," he continued.

I walked into the kitchen and made two mugs of coffee. I handed Mark his and asked him why he was thinking about Jews and forgiveness. He again was thoughtful for a few moments.

"I was really thinking about you and the relationship with your parents. After all, you did not see each other for twenty years following your baptism, did you?" he explained.

"Well, it's all blown over now," I sighed.

Unbeknown to me, during the months in 1974 when I was a patient in the Hospital for Tropical Diseases, London, my friend Helen made my parents an unexpected visit and told them in no uncertain terms about my illnesses, homelessness and financial situation. They did not, as she had hoped, make contact with me, but offered her a large amount of cash for my necessities, which she threw back at them.

My estranged parents received cards, for special occasions, weekly letters and birthday gifts from me. Nevertheless, I never heard from them. At one stage I wondered if they were dead, but Naomi, an old school chum, informed me that they were fairly fit and well. Only my maternal grandfather had died.

About six weeks before our wedding day which took place in Yorkshire on the 20th of August, 1983, Mark and I sent Mum and Dad an invitation. After five weeks we heard nothing, and so I decided to take the bull by the horns, as it were, and telephone them for their reply. I did not know what reception I would receive and I felt more than a little apprehensive. I took several deep breaths and dialled their number.

"Hello," came my dad's voice. "Hello ... who's there?"

After several moments I choked over a reply.

"Dad, please don't hang up on me? It's me, Becky."

There followed an awkward silence, but at least he kept on the line.

"Dad, I'm telephoning to ask if you and Mum will be able to attend our wedding. Please come."

He said no more to me but I heard him call my mother to the telephone.

"Hello, Becky," said my mother's surprisingly friendly voice, just as if we had never been apart for twenty years, which left me dumb-struck!

"Mum, please come to the wedding. It would be lovely for Mark and me if you came. Also, I need to inform the caterers regarding the seating plans! I'd like to buy you some flowers, too," I babbled.

"Please telephone us on Tuesday. We'll let you know then. If we do come you know that we cannot take a prominent part; you know that," she added, firmly.

During the afternoon of the following Tuesday, the Tuesday before 'the day', another telephone call confirmed the fact that they would attend our wedding!

It seemed strange to see them and they looked a little awkward and somewhat uncomfortable, remaining very much in the shadows.

I gave my mother a small spray of flowers. She accepted them without any words of thanks, but attempted a smile towards me as she turned to fuss around the young pageboy, making sure that the nine-year-old kept clean! No intimate conversations about the past and our present reunion took place on that day. There were no post-mortems.

"Well, you must have been pleased when they attended our wedding. I know I was," interjected Mark.

Of course, I was delighted.

"You say it has all 'blown over'. Have you let it pass or have you truly, truly forgiven them?" he asked, peering over his reading glasses at me.

"It is a thing of the past and, obviously, I completely understand why they behaved as they did," I replied. "It was something else with which I found it hard to come to terms."

Mark looked quizzical, egging me on to explain further.

"During Dad's time in the death camps Mother received a telegram from the War Office saying that he was 'missing, believed killed'. After a further year of silence she came to terms with being a war widow and free of her marriage. In 1945 Mum met one other man and they formed a relationship. It finished abruptly when she received a letter from Dad. Now it was in the October of 1978 that I was told my blood group - 'O' Positive. Dad's blood group is AB Negative. These mismatched blood groups proved to me that he could not be my natural father."

"You must have been horrified at the time," interrupted Mark.

I thought for a few moments and explained how I desperately wanted to know all about my real father, who he was, what he did. I said nothing, though, because maybe Mum had not informed Dad regarding her unfaithfulness to him. I did not wish to be the one to open up a can of worms. How could I be the one to dig up what happened all those years ago in 1945? It was just too long ago. Anyway, it is good to not only have them back as my parents, but as wonderful grandparents to our son Timothy.

I remember when, in 1984, I told them I was pregnant. They expressed great surprise that Mark and I, in our 'advancing years', should have actually planned to be parents! Nevertheless, they were more than overjoyed when, in the August of that year, Mark telephoned Mum and Dad informing them that it was a boy. (A boy is regarded by Jews as God's blessing on a family.)

"A son! When can you bring him to see us?" they shouted excitedly down the telephone.

When Timothy was just six weeks old the three of us motored down from Yorkshire to the south of England where my parents live. How very strange it seemed for us to enter their new home for the first time.

My maternal grandfather had died very shortly following my baptism in 1963. His apparently expected death suddenly freed my parents from his more than zealous religious discipline which he fanatically enforced upon them throughout their married life. He said that it was Ultra-Orthodoxy or nothing!

Anyway, after his death they decided to sell the very large family home and move to a more compact one which was situated way outside the familiar Jewish area. Living in an area where Jews and other ethnic races were virtually unknown they began to experience anti-Semitic hostility, the details of which they refused to reveal to me. Because of this they decided to openly deny their Jewishness, although their looks and mannerisms invariably give the game away!

During the time in October, 1984, when we were guests in their home they were very courteous to us, strangely never mentioning the twenty years when they disowned me. However, the then six-week-old Timothy became the apple of their eyes.

"Let me hold him now," pleaded my dad. "It's my turn."

"Later! He's comfortable with me just now," replied Mother, hugging the baby even closer.

"Well, he's just been sick on your shoulder!" laughed Dad.

Mark, having finished his coffee, yawned, indicating that it was time for bed, when, just then, our telephone rang. It was Dad.

"Hello, Becky, sorry to ring so late, but it is our wedding anniversary next month. It would be lovely if you and Mark joined us for a special meal. Bring Timothy too.

After all, he is seven years old now and he is so well behaved, isn't he? He'd enjoy the occasion!"

"As long as kosher pork is on the menu!" I joked.

He laughed.

It is wonderful to be reconciled with my family and I thank God for it. However, back in 1963 the Lord gave me a *firm* promise from Ezekiel 11:19. He said that He would give my parents a new heart and a new mind. He would take away their stubborn heart of stone and give them an obedient heart - a heart *fully* surrendered to Him. There is little doubt in my mind that God has begun a great change in them already. I now look forward to the time when they welcome Yeshua the Messiah. And they will, for when God speaks things happen.